FRANK BETTGER'S

HOW I RAISED MYSELF FROM FAILURE TO SUCCESS IN SELLING

FRANK BETTGER'S

HOW I RAISED MYSELF FROM FAILURE TO SUCCESS IN SELLING

A MODERN-DAY INTERPRETATION
OF A SELF-HELP CLASSIC
BY KAREN McCREADIE

Copyright © Infinite Ideas Limited, 2010
The right of Karen McCreadie to be identified as the author of this book has been asserted in accordance with the Copyright, Designs and Patents Act 1988.

First published in 2010 by
Infinite Ideas Limited
36 St Giles
Oxford, OX1 3LD
United Kingdom
www.infideas.com

A CIP catalogue record for this book is available from the British Library

ISBN 978–1–906821–31–9

Brand and product names are trademarks or registered trademarks of their respective owners.

Designed and typeset by Cylinder

BRILLIANT IDEAS

 INTRODUCTION

I must confess that I owned Bettger's *How I Raised Myself from Failure to Success in Selling* for years before I finally got around to reading it.

It was about sales, after all. I've read more books on sales than I care to mention and I have yet to be pleasantly surprised by any. Everything that there is to say on the subject has been said on the subject a million times before. So I was thrilled to find that Bettger's book is every bit as good as its reputation suggests. What makes this little book a revelation is not necessarily exactly what he says but the authenticity of the message. I don't know what Bettger looked like but he was sixty-one when he wrote the book, and it has the air of a kindly grandfather passing on hard-won lessons.

It is a conversation between you and a man who found success in what is, as far as I'm concerned, one of the hardest professions in the world.

Sales has, in the years since he wrote it, been elevated to an art form with books and theories about how to get past 'gatekeepers', how to sell to CEOs and how to get repeat business. Every conceivable angle has been covered. And yet, despite the sophistication that has emerged, we still instinctively know when we're being sold to – which, ironically, makes his authentic and simple approach even more relevant in the modern world.

So if you are looking for a turn-key, do-nothing, minimal-investment approach to selling then this book (or the original that inspired it) is not for you. There is nothing easy about what Bettger recommends. It is, for the most part, simple, but it's not easy.

How I Raised Myself from Failure to Success in Selling was first published in 1947. And despite the advances in technology and the emergence of a global marketplace since then, nothing much has changed at all. You and I don't buy from businesses – we buy from people. There is no such thing as business-2-business selling – it's just a buzz phrase that makes people in business feel as though they can approach selling with a little more finesse. Just think about it for a moment. If you are a buyer in a business, do you have preferred suppliers? If you are honest, do you choose those preferred suppliers based on price – or on price, quality and personality? I defy anyone to tell me it's all about the money. It's never about the money, not when you break it down. I remember when I used to work as a senior project manager for a marketing agency. Part of my role was to co-ordinate the printing and distribution of direct mail campaigns. I always got three quotes from a variety of suppliers, but the final decision rarely came down to price alone. It was about the relationships I had with those suppliers. Which ones did I like? Which suppliers were willing to go out on a limb for me and fix things without a fight? Who could I phone up and ask questions of without being made to feel like an idiot? Who did I laugh with? Those were the issues that made the difference!

These are people issues, not business-2-business – and that's what makes Bettger's advice timeless.

Selling offers an unprecedented opportunity for security and financial reward, and you don't need a university degree to excel in it. If you are good at sales you will never be out of work and you can effectively write your own salary cheque. And Bettger tells you how to be really good in sales.

1 LAZY GETS YOU NOWHERE

Before his career in sales Bettger was a professional baseball player. It was 1907 and he was playing for Johnstown, Pennsylvania in the Tri-State league. He was young and ambitious and yet he got fired. Confused by this turn of events, he asked his manager why – and was told he was lazy!

DEFINING IDEA...

If you aren't fired up with enthusiasm, you'll be fired with enthusiasm.

~ VINCE LOMBARDI,
AMERICAN FOOTBALL COACH

Bettger's team manager told him, 'You drag yourself around the field like a veteran who has been playing ball for twenty years. Why do you act this way if you are not lazy?'

Frank confided in his manager that he was actually nervous and his bravado and indifference was his way of hiding it. He didn't want the crowd or his teammates to know how scared he was, and he thought that if he took it easy he would be able to build up his confidence and get rid of his nerves.

Clearly the plan backfired.

Having the right attitude and working hard is perhaps more important now than ever before. I remember speaking to this horrible man one evening; he worked in the same place as my husband does. He was talking about how he did exactly what Bettger had done – he was lazy and did the absolute minimum that he could get away with. Although he never admitted it was due to fear, mind – no, it was always the company's fault, they didn't deserve his loyalty or commitment, blah, blah, blah…

When the recession hit there were some inevitable job losses. Who do you think they let go? Yep, you guessed it – that man and some others, many of whom never pulled their weight either. There are millions of people with a mindset like this in companies all over the world, and a recession is often a painful lesson about the dangers of being half-arsed about what you do. I'm not saying that all those who are made redundant deserve it – sometimes it has nothing to do with performance and the business concerned is just in serious trouble. Sadly, many good people also lose their jobs in a recession. But there can be no doubt that the first people added to the redundancy list are the lazy ones, those who have the poorest attitude and consistently deliver below-average performance. None of us are owed a living and to assume otherwise is a mistake.

Bettger's baseball manager gave him a priceless insight into how he was perceived by others and told him, 'It will never work. That's the thing that is holding you down. Whatever you do after you leave here, for heaven's sake, wake yourself up, and put some life and enthusiasm into your work!' We would all do well to take his advice.

HERE'S AN IDEA FOR YOU…

If you are fired, made redundant or are unsuccessful in winning a new piece of business, ask why. Explain that you would genuinely like some feedback and be sure to give the other person permission for total honesty. You won't always like what you hear, but it may offer you some insight that could help you in the future. If you never ask you will simply jump to conclusions that could perpetuate the situation.

2 ACT AS IF

Bettger took his ex-manager's advice to heart and managed to get a trial with New Haven, Connecticut. 'From the minute I appeared on the field I acted like a man electrified. I acted as though I were alive with a million batteries... Did it work? It worked like magic.'

Bettger admits that it was all an act. He didn't really feel electrified but he pretended that he did, even though it was nearly 100°F that day. What he discovered was that:

- His enthusiasm overcame his fear and nerves almost completely. In fact, he realised that they worked for him as he played better than he had ever thought possible.

- His enthusiasm was infectious, and the other players in his team became more enthusiastic too.

- The heat didn't affect him – he felt better than ever.

DEFINING IDEA...

If you want a quality, act as if you already had it. Try the 'as if' technique.
– WILLIAM JAMES, AMERICAN PSYCHOLOGIST AND PHILOSOPHER

The reason why this worked is because the mind does not know the difference between something real and something imagined. Maxwell Maltz, a psychologist and plastic surgeon, wrote in his groundbreaking book *Psycho-Cybernetics*, 'Experimental and clinical psychologists have proven beyond a shadow of a doubt that the human nervous system cannot tell the difference between an "actual" experience and an experience imagined vividly and in detail.'

What this means is that if you pretend to have a certain emotion, such as confidence or enthusiasm, then the mind and body will create the conditions of confidence and enthusiasm. It is therefore possible for you to act as if you have a particular trait and, in the process, create that trait. Now, this doesn't mean you can imagine that you can drive a car, and that this means you actually can drive a car – there are physical skills involved that you actually need to learn. But you already know how to be enthusiastic or confident. These are intangible states, not skills.

Emotions such as enthusiasm have a particular chemical signature. The mind and body work together to create the environment for enthusiasm and either can trigger it. If you are excited about something, then the body will release a cocktail of chemicals including endorphins and you will feel that feeling. What is less understood is that we can trigger that same response mentally, by pretending to feel that emotion, and because the mind doesn't know the difference between reality and imagination it will create the same result. You therefore have much more control over how you feel than you may realise.

Bettger's biggest thrill was a report in the local paper the next morning which said, 'This new player, Bettger, has a barrel of enthusiasm. He inspired our boys.' His enthusiasm increased his income by 700% in just ten days and he multiplied his income thirty times over the following two years!

HERE'S AN IDEA FOR YOU...

If you are going for a job interview or have an important meeting or some major event to attend and you don't feel up to it, change your mind. Listening to upbeat music and dancing around the living room for five minutes is a simple way to break out of a bad mood in a hurry. Then just fake it – pretend you are auditioning for the role of your life.

3 FIND THE OPPORTUNITY IN ADVERSITY

While playing a baseball game against the Chicago Cubs, 'something snapped' in Bettger's arm and he was forced to retire from baseball. Bettger said, 'This seemed like a great tragedy to me at the time but now I look back on it as one of the most fortunate events of my life.'

DEFINING IDEA...

Adversity has the effect of eliciting talents, which in prosperous circumstances would have lain dormant.

~ HORACE

The hard thing about finding opportunity in adversity is that it only becomes clear when you are able to look back on the situation. We rarely have the capacity to foresee that opportunity. It's very difficult, for example, to be made redundant and immediately swing around and find anything positive about that, especially when you have a mortgage to pay and three kids at home.

It's hard to be dumped by the love of your life and have your friends tell you that there will be someone better around the corner. It may well be true, but having the emotional intelligence, perspective and strength to pursue that opportunity or go searching for it isn't so easy.

I can't imagine that Lance Armstrong was thrilled when he was diagnosed with testicular cancer and given a fifty-fifty chance of survival. Yet he went on to win the Tour de France seven times and become an inspiration to millions – and he maintains that cancer was the best thing that ever happened to him.

I always remember a story I heard that has helped me to rummage around in the unhappy or difficult events of my life, and it may also help you. If your house burned down, would you return to the smoking debris and scratch through the rubble to see if there was anything you could salvage? Would you look for photographs or letters, heirlooms or trinkets – anything of either emotional or financial value? Of course you would. If you knew there was a three-carat diamond in that house and that it therefore couldn't have been destroyed by the fire, would you be on your hands and knees for a fortnight trying to find it? Yes, you probably would. So why do we treat setbacks and life's inevitable adversities any differently?

Things will always go wrong, life will always rise up from time to time and slap us in the face – it's the nature of the beast. So why would we not take a moment to compose ourselves at those times, and go ferreting around for something good or an opportunity for something even better?

There are, of course, occasions that render this philosophy useless. The death of a loved one or a violent crime are two examples where no amount of searching for a positive element will deliver one. There is no diamond in the dust in those situations, but for everything else there probably is. At least it's worth a look.

HERE'S AN IDEA FOR YOU...

Look back on your life and choose one situation or event that, at the time, rocked you to the core. With the passage of time are you able to see any advantages that came from that situation? Who did you meet, where did you go and what did you do as a direct result of it? Did any of those things work out well? With hindsight some of our most challenging times prove to be a springboard to something better.

4 THE POWER OF COINCIDENCE

Following his baseball career Bettger started work selling life insurance and hated every minute of it. This period was 'the longest and most disheartening months of my life'.

In order to improve he enrolled in Dale Carnegie's public-speaking course and was able to recognise a recurring theme, a coincidence that would alter his life.

DEFINING IDEA...

I like coincidences. They make me wonder about destiny, and whether free will is an illusion or just a matter of perspective. They let me speculate on the idea of some master plan that, from time to time, we're allowed to see out the corner of our eye.

~ CHUCK SIGARS, WRITER

In his previous role as a baseball player Bettger had once been fired for his lack of enthusiasm. When he enrolled in the public-speaking course he was immediately met with the exact same criticism. When he gave his first presentation, Dale Carnegie interrupted his efforts, adding, 'Why don't you talk with a little enthusiasm?'

Later that evening Bettger realised that, 'the very fault which had threatened to wreck my career in baseball was now threatening to wreck my career as a salesman'. It is this type of coincidence that I believe often holds the biggest opportunity for growth.

If something happens once in your life then you can put it down to luck or chance. If the same thing happens twice, like the situation with Bettger's lack of enthusiasm, then it is probably not luck or chance but a sign that you need to get ready for change. This isn't the result of life just unfolding in a completely random fashion – it could be an invitation to change. If exactly that same event happens three times or more then you definitely need to change.

There are lots of examples. Say, for instance, that you find yourself in similar relationships over and over again... Or if you change jobs frequently, and miraculously find that your complaint about the last boss is the same complaint you now have about the new boss – well, then it's time to wake up to the possibility that the problem might not be the boss; it might be you. If you find that you are always the first to go in an economic downturn and have been made redundant half a dozen times there may be some clues in there for you. These things are not haphazard, strange quirks of nature or fascinating coincidences, they are an opportunity for you to step back and assess where you might need to change. There is no such thing as a meaningless coincidence.

Fortunately, Bettger was able to see the pattern and acted immediately to break the cycle. He writes, 'I shall never forget the first call I made the next day. It was my first "crashing through" session. I made up my mind that I was going to show my prospect the most enthusiastic salesman he'd ever seen in his life.' And the 'magic of enthusiasm' worked for him again – but only because he was able to spot his own particular pattern through coincidence and make the necessary adjustments.

HERE'S AN IDEA FOR YOU...

Take a moment to review the last five years of your life. Are there any similarities between the people you meet, the relationships you get involved in? Can you spot any recurring themes? If you can, then act on the information and alter your approach.

5 ANCHOR ENTHUSIASM INTO THE WAY YOU OPERATE

Bettger raises an important issue: 'Can you acquire enthusiasm or must you be born with it?' Modern science and our understanding of the mind/body connection have proved what Bettger believed to be true – you can definitely acquire it. We can 'act as if' or use a more structured approach of affirmations and anchoring.

Frank tells the story of how a man called Stanley Gettis became a 'human dynamo'. He achieved this by reciting a poem every morning for twenty years! The poem acted as an affirmation and triggered the necessary emotion through a process known in neurolinguistic programming (or NLP) as anchoring.

DEFINING IDEA...

You can do anything if you have enthusiasm... Enthusiasm is at the bottom of all progress. With it, there is accomplishment. Without it, there are only alibis.
– HENRY FORD

First, affirmations. It was Émile Coué who first wrote about the power of affirmation in his little book called *Self Mastery Through Conscious Autosuggestion*, originally published in 1922. Coué makes reference to the fact that we have 'two absolutely distinct selves within us'. Both are intelligent, but one is conscious and the other is unconscious. Autosuggestion is the process where we use the conscious mind to imprint on the unconscious mind to effect change. Autosuggestion often takes the form of affirmations that you recite with enthusiasm through the day. If you've ever come across the rather trite suggestion to laminate positive statements and put them in the shower, then you have come across an affirmation technique.

This repetition of positive affirmation is said to overwrite any negative imprint in the subconscious mind to effect change. Personally, I've never used affirmations for longer than a day or so. I get bored, and the more I learn about the subconscious mind the more I question whether anything stored there can really be overwritten by repeating positive statements over and over and over again. I think it's a little simplistic and naive.

A continuation of this idea and theme is the NLP technique of anchoring. An anchor is just a stimulus that evokes a consistent response. You will have probably heard of Pavlov's dogs. In this experiment ringing a bell was connected to the dogs being fed so that eventually the sound of the bell (the stimulus) was all that was needed for the dogs to salivate (the consistent response). It then becomes a conditioned response, and anchoring allows you to do the same for enthusiasm.

However you do manage to achieve it, find a way to embody relentless enthusiasm in all that you do. At the close of Bettger's first chapter, Dale Carnegie urges the reader to 'reread many times this chapter by Frank Bettger, and to make a high and holy resolve that you will double the amount of enthusiasm that you have been putting into your work and into your life. If you carry out that resolve, you will probably double your income and double your happiness.'

HERE'S AN IDEA FOR YOU...

Anchoring is a standard NLP technique. If you would like to know how to create positive anchors so you can quickly and easily muster up helpful emotions at will, then search the Internet for 'How to create an NLP anchor' and you will be given thousands of sites that will teach you the process. Or you could seek out a master practitioner in your area.

6 IF YOU WANT TO IMPROVE SOMETHING – MEASURE IT

In his second chapter Bettger discusses the single phrase that put him back into selling after he'd quit. That sentence was, 'The business of selling narrows down to one thing – just one thing … seeing the people.' And the only way to ensure that it happened was to set targets and keep accurate records.

DEFINING IDEA...

Evaluate what you want – because what gets measured, gets produced.

~ JAMES A. BELASCO, AUTHOR

He heard the inspirational words from his previous boss, Mr Talbot, who happened to be delivering a team pep talk as Bettger was in the office to collect his things. Mr Talbot went on to say, 'Show me a man of ordinary ability who will go out and earnestly tell his story to four or five people every day and I will show you a man who just can't help making good!' Bettger realised the simple truth of his words and wrote that 'it was just as though the sun had suddenly burst out from the clouds'.

Re-inspired by the simplicity of the message, Bettger went back to work. Taking Mr Talbot's message literally, he began to keep a record of the number of calls he made. Initially this was just to make sure that he did what was necessary to ensure that he saw those four or five people every day.

In the process Bettger discovered a few interesting things that salespeople have been discovering ever since. The first is that often the simplest advice is the best, although simple rarely means easy! Plus, human beings have a tendency to lie to themselves. You know what I mean – those little deals you make with yourself to justify not having to call on someone or the conviction with which you tell yourself that the paperwork is every bit as important as making appointments. By keeping score, Bettger was forced to remove the rose-coloured glasses and see – honestly – just how few people he had been meeting before.

In the following ten weeks he sold more than he had done in the previous ten months. As his confidence grew, so did his appreciation for his time. In an effort to waste as little as possible he decided he didn't need to keep a record of the calls he made any more, and his sales fell away again.

It's all very well having targets and goals but if we don't take the time to measure them human nature will step in and fudge the figures. If we want to change any habit or behaviour, we have to describe the exact nature of that change together with a detailed map of how we intend to get there. Measuring something doesn't necessarily mean it will get done. But if we don't measure it, it almost certainly won't. As Bettger says 'Without records we have no way of knowing what we are doing wrong.'

HERE'S AN IDEA FOR YOU...

Think of something you want to change just now. Do you have a clear picture of what the ideal situation is? Do you have an incremental plan of action about how it will come about, what small changes need to be made in order to arrive at the outcome? Break the change down into small measurable chunks, do them – and measure them!

7 DEVIL'S IN THE DETAIL

Following Bettger's return to record keeping, his sales soared. A year later he stood before his agency and shared his detailed records. He says, 'I had secretly kept records of my calls for twelve months.' This detail offered great insight which increased his productivity even further.

He had made 1849 calls. From those calls he had interviewed 828 people and closed 65 sales. His commission on those sales was $4,251.82. Armed with that detail, he was able to calculate that every call had made him $2.30.

This information changed his whole outlook: 'Now, every call I made, regardless of whether I saw the man or not, put $2.30 in my pocket!'

DEFINING IDEA...

Men who wish to know about the world must learn about it in its particular details

– HERACLITUS, GREEK PHILOSOPHER

The detailed records allowed him to shift his perspective and see those calls as valuable. He wasn't discouraged by rejection any more. Far from it; each call that he made put money in his pocket. They say that sales is a numbers game and it's true. It's a numbers game because you will succeed if you just keep making the calls; if you keep seeing the people and doing your presentation and asking for the sale you will make the sales. Sure, it will help if you have the hide of a rhinoceros as rejection is the staple diet of those in sales. But if you just keep making the calls you'll make the sales and make the money.

It's also a numbers game because numbers give you power. Bettger was able to use the insights he gained from the accurate record he kept to lift his spirits when he was down. And he was even able to take it one step further; over time he was able to increase the value of each call from $2.30 to $19.00.

His record told him that 70% of his sales were made on the first interview, 23% on the second and only 7% on the third or later. This knowledge allowed him to turn his focus to where it mattered – only the first and second interviews.

There is a myth in business that all customers are good customers – but they are not. Some are just a pain in the arse. But if you don't know one from the other then you risk wasting time on people who eat up your time and cause nothing but grief. Remember the Pareto principle, which says that 80% of the sales come from 20% of the customers. If that is true, then why waste your time on the customers who do not yield the greatest reward?

Bettger reminds us that keeping records can give us a new way of looking at our 'failures' and also help us separate the wheat from the chaff in selling.

HERE'S AN IDEA FOR YOU...

Stop wasting time on tyre-kickers. In order to do that you need to work out where your business comes from. Who are your best customers? Consider how easy and enjoyable they are to deal with, how quickly they pay and whether or not they refer you to other people. Do these people have any similarities or belong in certain industries? Find the similarities and research where you could find more people like them.

8 JUST DO IT!

Bettger tells the story of a baseball player called Steve Evans who played with him when he played for the Cardinals. Apparently he was every bit as good as Babe Ruth apart from one thing: 'The habit of waiting. He usually had two strikes called on him before he began swinging.'

DEFINING IDEA...
You can't hit 'em if you don't swing at 'em.
~ CLAY W. HAMLIN, SALESMAN

In one particularly important game it was Steve's turn to bat, and 'any kind of hit would have won the game'. True to form, two strikes. The manager shouted from the dugout, 'Evans – what the hell yuh waitin' for?' Evans yelled back in disgust, 'The first and the fifteenth, watta yuh think?' Those were pay days.

Even though baseball is a US sport you won't have heard of Evans. Why? Because despite having the talent and hitting power of a legend like Babe Ruth he had a lousy attitude and wouldn't take the opportunities that were presented to him.

Whether you are trying to succeed in sales or trying to pluck up enough courage to ask someone out on a date, take Nike's advice and 'just do it'. Take a risk. Sure you might end up looking foolish or you might be rejected, but at least you'll know one way or the other.

Sitting around waiting for the perfect time is also the perfect recipe for disappointment. There is no such thing as the perfect time – there is just right now. Procrastination and perfectionism are just fear wrapped up in a different coat to make the people wearing them feel better about themselves: 'Oh, but I'm a perfectionist, I want to get it just right.' No you don't – you're so terrified of getting it wrong that you'd rather procrastinate a little longer. Be honest and get on with what needs to be done. Stop worrying about the possible outcome and just do it now – and then you'll know the outcome. Certainty has power to it. Even a certain 'no' is better than hovering in indecision.

Even if, like me, you can't understand how a sport that is only played in the US can possibly have a world series, you will probably still have heard of Babe Ruth. The record books are quick to point out his unapproachable total of 714 home runs. What you may not know is that he also holds the record for striking out more times than any other player in history! He failed 1330 times. Ironically, it's that record that sets him apart in the history books. History remembers those with the courage to give 100% every time.

Bettger concluded, 'Selling is the easiest job in the world if you work at it hard – but the hardest job in the world if you try to work it easy.'

HERE'S AN IDEA FOR YOU...

Think of something you have been putting off for a while. Write a list, right now, of the pros and cons of taking action. Look at the list and if the pros outweigh the cons then do whatever it is – now. Obviously, if what you've been putting off for a while is robbing the local bank and you subsequently take my advice then, for the record, I take absolutely no responsibility for you being an idiot!

9 SPEAK YOUR WAY TO SUCCESS

Being able to communicate your product or service offering confidently and with enthusiasm is a key aspect of success in selling. Bettger suggests, 'I would urge any man or woman who is being held back by fear, and who lacks courage and self-confidence, to join the best public-speaking course in his or her community.'

Communication is the key to everything – not just success in sales. Being able to express yourself in a confident manner is essential for happy relationships, good parenting, leadership roles – and will very often determine how far up an organisation you will progress.

DEFINING IDEA...

Great is our admiration of the orator who speaks with fluency and discretion.

– CICERO

Bettger tells his readers how he would tie himself in knots when he had to talk to prospects and how his fears and lack of confidence would be transferred to the product or service he was trying to sell, making it virtually impossible for him to do well. So he enrolled in a public speaking course run by Dale Carnegie. Today most people have heard of Dale Carnegie, as he went on to become extremely well known as a speaker and author of the famous little book, *How to Win Friends and Influence People*.

For anyone who has ever worked in sales one question invariably pops up: 'Are good salespeople born or made?' I think it's both. Some people are just born with the gift of the gab and can talk to anyone about anything. My dad was a bit like that – it didn't matter where he went, he would strike up a conversation with someone.

Then there are the rest of us, and we have to try a little harder.

In the last decade or so weekend seminars and training programmes have become popular in the UK and overseas. It's big business, and the format is usually quite similar. You go to a presentation – often a free information night – where you are then encouraged to attend a weekend event, and in this weekend event you are on-sold to some high-end products and services. It is a very powerful format and one that is made possible by those proficient in public speaking; I often ghost-write for speakers who have found that a book is the ultimate business card and can increase their profile. Gaining confidence in public speaking will not only increase your ability to sell, extend your reach and centres of influence, but it may also lead you down new and lucrative career paths.

Bettger does, however, make one caveat with reference to the type of course you should attend: 'Don't join just any lecture course. Join only a course where you make a talk at every meeting, because that's what you want – experience in speaking.' The best way to learn anything is to actually do it, not talk about doing it!

HERE'S AN IDEA FOR YOU...

If there is no appropriate course in your own community, do what Benjamin Franklin did with the creation of the 'Junto' – form your own. Ask around to find a group of like-minded people who want to improve their public-speaking skills and enhance their self-confidence. Meet each week and practise presenting to the group, critique each other and keep on presenting.

10 SELF-ORGANISATION

Not long after Bettger began to keep records he discovered his self-organisation skills were not great. He confesses: 'My intentions were good. I kept making new resolutions but they never lasted very long. I just couldn't get organised.' We've all had this experience where resolve gives way to excuses.

Most people recoil at the idea of strict schedules with every moment accounted for. Bettger pre-empts his readers' reluctance but reminds us that, 'You are already living on a schedule. And if it's not a planned one, it's probably a poor one.'

According to Bettger, the great industrialist Henry L. Doherty said, 'I can hire men to do everything but two things, think and do things in the order of their importance.'

DEFINING IDEA...
Never begin the day until it is finished on paper.
– JIM ROHN, AUTHOR AND SPEAKER

It's easy in business, and especially in sales, to procrastinate over the tasks you don't want to do or don't like doing, such as calling prospects. It's easy to decide to shuffle papers instead of picking up the phone, especially on a Friday afternoon.

Bettger suggests, however, that planning your time is as critical to success as measuring your activity. Time management is a huge concern for business owners as they struggle to get the best out of themselves and their people. This quandary has been around for a long time.

In the 1920s Ivy Lee, the man considered to be the father of modern public relations, was called in to help Charles Schwab with a challenge he had. Schwab wanted to know how to make his managers at Bethlehem Steel more effective with their time. The story goes that Lee offered to give Schwab the secret to time management and solve his problem then and there. All he had to do was implement the system for one week and then send him a cheque for what he thought it was worth.

Lee advised Schwab to have his managers list their top six priorities for the following day at the end of every day. They were then asked to rank the list in order of importance with the most important in position one and the least important in position six. At the start of each day, the managers were to work on the number one priority until it was complete or no further action could be taken, and then move to priority two and repeat the process.

Within a couple of weeks Schwab voluntarily sent Lee a cheque for $25,000, which in today's terms would be a cheque for $250,000! Obviously it worked…

Planning your day is critical to success. As Bettger points out, 'I prefer to work on a tight schedule four and a half days a week and get somewhere than to be working all the time and never get anywhere.'

HERE'S AN IDEA FOR YOU…

If you are struggling to get everything done or find time to adequately plan your schedule Bettger suggests you join the 'Six o'clock Club'. As the name would suggest, you get up at 6 a.m. (I can vouch for this approach, although I'm not much fun after a week of it.) Apparently Benjamin Franklin said that only a few men live to old age and fewer still ever become successful who are not early risers — clearly that's where I've been going wrong!

11 FIND OUT WHAT PEOPLE WANT AND HELP THEM GET IT

Following a particularly large sale Clayton M. Hunsicker, a nationally known salesman of the time, congratulated Bettger and explained how it had been possible: 'The most important secret of salesmanship is to find out what the other fellow wants, then help him find the best way to get it.'

DEFINING IDEA...

The highest service we can perform for others is to help them help themselves.

~ HORACE MANN,
AMERICAN EDUCATION REFORMER

At this time Bettger was pretty green in the world of sales; he had never finished school and was by his own admission a 'blundering dud'. Yet despite these self-imposed limitations he had sold life insurance to a hard-nosed business executive and left the office with a cheque for $8672, which was the first year's premium. Bettger doesn't say when this happened, but considering that the book was published in 1947 it was a significant investment for a novice salesman to secure.

His success caused a 'mild sensation' and he was invited to tell his story at the national sales conference. Hunsicker had come up to him after his presentation to congratulate him. He smiled at Bettger and said, 'I still doubt whether you understand exactly why you were able to make the sale.' What he had done was stumble accidentally across the most important secret of salesmanship.

When you focus on the other person and find out their hopes and dreams so that you can help them achieve those things, the dynamic changes completely.

It stops being about what you can sell someone and becomes about how you can help them achieve their objective.

For example, I am a professional ghost writer as well as an author. I write for busy professionals, CEOs and international speakers who recognise the business and product development opportunities that a book presents. My clients don't dream of a finished manuscript; they dream of a book in their hands – one they can give to their friends, family and prospective customers, sign at a local bookshop and be able to buy on Amazon. So I will write the book but I will also ensure they understand the publishing process, the pros and cons of each publishing option. I will also introduce them to publishing contacts, editors, proofreaders and designers so they can fully realise their ambition.

Bettger says that this simple insight changed the way he looked at selling forever. He says, 'Before this, I had largely thought of selling as just a way of making a living for myself. I had dreaded to go in to see people, for I fear I was making a nuisance of myself. But now, I was inspired! I resolve right then to dedicate the rest of my selling career to this principle: Finding out what people want, and helping them get it.' We may all do well to do the same.

HERE'S AN IDEA FOR YOU...

Instead of working out what you can get from the transaction or what sort of commissions or benefit you will receive from the sale, focus on finding out what your customers truly want and make it your job to help them get it. Sometimes that will mean no benefit for you at all – but there are few people who are prepared to help others for no benefit so you will stand out from the crowd.

12 KEEP ON LEARNING

Ongoing learning is critical to success: 'Top salesmen are all hungry for new ideas and always hunting for ways to do their job better. Attend as many sales conventions as you can. If you get only one idea, the time and money you spend will be the best investment you'll ever make.'

This mythology about only having to get one good idea to validate the investment in time and money is still alive and well in the seminar industry today. The exact same line is used in glossy brochures and training advertisements, and yet the reality is slightly different.

DEFINING IDEA...

Anyone who keeps learning stays young. The greatest thing in life is to keep our mind young.

~ HENRY FORD

We are led to believe that once we have this fantastic new idea then the implementation of it will be a breeze. Only it's not. Contrary to popular belief, turning an idea into action is not an innate skill that everyone has. If it was, no one would be overweight, everyone would go to the gym three times a week and we'd actually be using that 'new' customer database that was installed three years ago.

There is now some evidence emerging from the science of the brain that there is a biological link to this trait and that some people are therefore more inclined to convert ideas into action than others. The basal ganglia in the midbrain is responsible for integrating thoughts and feelings with physical actions. Scientists have proven that 'doers' actually have more basal ganglia activity than most people.

So if you often attend seminars or training courses and leave full of exuberance and life-changing proclamations only to irritate your friends and family for a fortnight and then revert to 'normal', or if you have umpteen brilliant ideas scribbled in notebooks or on the back of airplane boarding passes, napkins or the margins of books – don't despair. You just need to create a framework to help you consciously manage that transition from idea to action. You need to sit down and plan the individual steps that need to happen to make it a reality, otherwise it probably won't happen.

If you want to stay abreast of the new innovations and ideas in your industry, then you have to view your education as an ongoing lifelong pursuit and in that respect Hunsicker was right. But that training and learning must be tempered with activity, otherwise it's pointless. It will lull you into a false sense of security because you'll think you are making progress, whereas in reality you're soothing your ego and nothing more.

If you attend high-quality conferences and find the very best training, then the experience provides added benefits. They 'will give you an opportunity to meet some of the big fellows. Meeting them personally and hearing them talk will inspire you. You'll go back home with a new confidence and enthusiasm.'

HERE'S AN IDEA FOR YOU...

Attend conferences and training seminars but make a pact with yourself that you are only allowed to attend another one when you have demonstrated action on at least one idea from the previous investment. In addition, make sure the training you attend is provided by people who are actually doing what you do instead of those who did it thirty years ago and have since made their living from running seminars!

13 DON'T TALK ABOUT YOURSELF

Talking about himself, Bettger writes about the 'same mistake that I had been making (and might have kept right on making all the rest of my life if it hadn't been for Clayt Hunsicker)'. If you want to sell anything, focus all your attention on what the other person wants and needs.

Bettger tells of being approached to speak at a local sales school. The first request was made by a Mr Brown, who told Bettger he had spent a great deal on advertising and that they needed to attract a big crowd to ensure enough people signed up for the school and how he would be grateful for his help. Bettger declined.

A little later another man called with an entirely different proposition. He appealed to Bettger's desire to help other young salesmen: 'You know how much this same training would have meant to you when you were trying to get started.'

Needless to say, Bettger gave the second presentation – because the second request had been made entirely from his viewpoint.

This is not just a challenge in selling; it's rife in marketing too. Business owners spend hours honing their corporate messages for a promotional brochure or pore over copy for a website only to shoot themselves in the foot by banging on about themselves or their company for most of it. My personal favourite is 'We've been in business for twenty-five years!'

Seriously – who cares? The only reason people might care is if you can link that longevity back to your ability to solve their problems or make their lives better, easier, happier, safer or richer in some way. Your potential customers don't care what exciting new piece of equipment you've bought or who your 'new member of the team' is – unless you can demonstrate how it benefits them. They want to know what you can do for them, not the other way around.

We are being bombarded by sales messages all the time and, as a consequence, we are getting very skilled at ignoring the majority of them. In our house, for example, the TV mute button is in almost constant use. Don't waste time trying to tell people how great you are or how fantastic your products are; stop talking about yourself. Your task is to discover what your customers want and present yourself as the solution. Then, and only then, will your twenty-five years of expertise mean anything.

Bettger reminds us that 'there is only one way under high heaven to get anybody to do anything. Did you ever stop to think of that? Yes, just one way. And this is by making the other person want to do it. Remember there is no other way.'

HERE'S AN IDEA FOR YOU...

If you are preparing a presentation or writing marketing material constantly ask yourself this crucial question: 'Who cares?' If your presentation leaves the listener wondering 'so what?' then you need to revise it. Focus on what your product or service can do for your client. What problem do you solve or what benefit do you deliver? How will buying your product make their life better, easier, happier, safer or richer?

14 MAKE APPOINTMENTS AND BE PREPARED

According to Bettger the points raised in this and the following seven chapters constitute the perfect technique for selling and can be used in selling of all kinds from 'shoes and ships and sealing wax'. These principles constitute the essential elements of sales and can be used for anything.

Although this advice was written in 1947, it is perhaps even more valid now.

Bettger says, 'Be expected! You gain a big advantage when you make an appointment. It tells the other person you appreciate the value of his time. Unconsciously he places more importance on the value of your time.' This is still true today – only now you will rarely get in to see people without an appointment.

DEFINING IDEA...

Failing to plan is planning to fail.
~ ALAN LAKEIN, AUTHOR

And if you do, you probably won't be welcome. My brother is a farmer and I help him out from time to time. It's bloody hard work and I deeply respect anyone who can make a living from it, especially with all the red tape and mountains of legislation imposed from Brussels by people who have never even set foot on a farm. When I've been helping, salesmen have often arrived unannounced. Usually it is quite obvious – even to the untrained eye – that my brother is busy and yet they will hover about asking stupid questions such as 'are you busy just now?' or 'what's the weather been like?'

Needless to say, nothing is sold during these encounters. It's disrespectful to assume that you can visit someone without an appointment, or at least the permission to do so. It's also extremely annoying for the prospective client and annoyed people don't buy stuff. To make matters worse most of these unannounced salesmen are usually 'just passing'. There is no pitch, no solution to a challenge or answer to a pressing problem that is going to make my brother's life easier, safer or more enjoyable.

Which brings us to Bettger's second point – be prepared. He rightly points out that if you were asked to make a presentation to an important group of people for a significant fee then you would prepare: 'You'd sit up nights, planning exactly how you would open your talk; points you wanted to cover; your close. You'd treat it as an event, wouldn't you?' Bettger continues, 'Well, don't forget there is no difference between an audience of four hundred and an audience of one.'

Being prepared is not just about respecting your own and other people's time, it develops cast-iron confidence. If you know the points you wish to cover, how your product or service can add value, how you can solve a problem and are prepared for the inevitable objections, then you can tackle any situation.

HERE'S AN IDEA FOR YOU...

Don't give in to the temptation to prepare on the way to the meeting – your preparation will be rushed and inadequate. Do it the night before. Run through all scenarios ahead of time in your head so you can consider the possible outcomes. That way you are prepared. If you work in an industry where unannounced visits are still common at least have the decency to ask if it is a convenient time. If not, then make an alternative arrangement.

15 WHAT IS THE KEY ISSUE?

The best way to ensure you are properly prepared is to consider two questions. What is the major point of interest and what is the most vulnerable point? These questions allow you to focus on the big issues and see your product or service from your client's point of view.

This process does several things. First, it allows you to hone your message and reduce the time you need to get that message across. There are so many demands on our time in the modern world that everything has to matter and if you can provide solutions to genuine problems and allow someone to have a better, safer, healthier or happier life in some way then you have minutes (possibly seconds) to make your point.

One way to think about your offer is from the perspective of:

Problem – Aggravate – Solve

It's a simple way of looking at selling situations so that you keep on track and ensure you talk about things that will matter to your client and not to you. You want to know what is keeping your client up at night. What brings him or her out in a cold sweat? If you can uncover that fear or challenge and your product or service is a genuine solution for it, then selling should be easier.

If you are unsure, then go back to past clients and ask them why they bought from you. Ask them what their main concerns were and whether there was a key issue that tipped them into a 'yes'. Was there something you said that drove home the danger of not taking action right now?

Once you establish what your client's key issues are then you need to aggravate the problem. In Bettger's case, he sold life insurance so he would draw his clients' attention to the consequences of not taking action; he made them realise that every day without adequate insurance put both his client and his client's family in danger. After aggravating the situation you then present the solution which is, of course, your product or service.

All of this is only possible if you take the time to prepare and really try and appreciate your offering from your prospective client's point of view.

This idea of key issues is also central to good advertising. Advertising and selling that works both stick to one central idea or key issue and develop a case around that idea. Otherwise you risk confusing the prospect and confused people don't buy any more readily than annoyed people do. Keep it simple, find the 'hot buttons' – and press them.

Bettger reminds us, 'Never try to cover too many points; don't obscure the main issue. Find out what it is; then stay right on the beam.'

HERE'S AN IDEA FOR YOU...

Not everyone can immediately make the perfect presentation or make an important telephone call and remember all the points they want to cover in the correct order in the shortest amount of time. Create some key-word notes to help you stay on point. Review the notes immediately before the meeting – and should you get flustered in the meeting and forget anything, you have them at hand.

16 ASK QUESTIONS

After attending a sales conference in Philadelphia, Bettger heard one of America's top salesmen reveal the secret of effectively handling objections. Don't respond 'with smart stock answers found in books written about "How to Meet Objections".' Instead meet those objections by asking questions.

Bettger tells of how he sat, listening to the presentation and the demonstration from the stage, pop-eyed at just how effective it was. The speaker was a chap called Elliot Hall and, according to Bettger, 'No one got the impression that he was arguing or contradicting anybody. He was extremely forceful; yet never once did he argue, or contradict, or offer a fixed opinion of his own. His attitude was not that of 'I know I'm right; you're wrong.'

Having said that, the audience was full of salesmen – hardly your average audience. Anyway Bettger decided to give it a go and his unsuspecting guinea pig was a Mr Booth. He prepared fifteen questions and needed to ask eleven of them to close the sale.

According to Bettger, there are several advantages of asking questions. They help you to avoid getting into an argument with your prospective customer. Rather than telling someone what you think they should do, questions allow you to present your information in a more amenable fashion so that over time the prospect will take ownership of your idea. Questions also prevent you from talking too much and open up the communication. Bettger tells of seeing a young president of a construction business who was very definite in his refusal to speak to him. Bettger says, 'There was something so final in his manner, I felt as though it would be fatal to be persistent. So I ventured one question: "Mr Allen, how did you ever happen to get started in the building construction business?"' Bettger listened for three hours!

People love to talk about themselves. And when they do, you can pick up all sorts of information about what they want and how you can genuinely help them. Often we don't know what we think about something until we verbalise it to others. Asking questions therefore allows your prospect to crystallise their thinking and helps them to recognise what they need.

According to Bettger, a famous educator once told him, 'One of the biggest things you get out of a college education is a questioning attitude, a habit of demanding and weighing evidence … a scientific approach.' He continues to say that although he never went to college, 'I know one of the best ways to get men to think is to ask them questions. In fact, I have found in many cases it is the only way to get them to think!'

HERE'S AN IDEA FOR YOU...

Next time you are in an interview or sales meeting and it's not going well, consider asking some questions about how the other person got to the position he or she is now in. Remember this is probably a story they are quite proud of and yet their loved ones probably groan every time they mention it. A fresh pair of ears can be a welcome relief; all you have to do is listen and they'll think you're really interesting at the end!

17 EXPLODE DYNAMITE AND AROUSE FEAR

Bettger suggests that you do something unexpected and/ or arouse fear, adding, 'Basically there are only two factors that move men to action: desire for gain, and fear of loss. Advertising men tell us that fear is the most motivating factor where risk or danger is involved.'

DEFINING IDEA...

The most drastic, and usually the most effective, remedy for fear is direct action.

~ WILLIAM BURNHAM, AUTHOR

Social psychologist Robert B. Cialdini drew our attention to six basic principles of psychology that direct human behaviour in his brilliant book *Influence: Science and Practice*. One of those principles is scarcity. Scarcity is the idea that opportunities seem more valuable to us when they are less available.

Human beings hate to miss out – even if what we are missing out on is something that we normally wouldn't give two hoots about. As soon as there is a risk that we may not be able to buy something or that our access to something is limited in some way it suddenly becomes much more attractive. In addition there is an automatic assumption made about the quality of the offering – after all, if there are only a limited number left they must be good because they are selling fast!

A recent example of the lunacy of this principle in action was when Swiss watchmaker Romain Jerome launched the new 'Day & Night' watch. As the name would indicate, the watch didn't tell the time – just whether it was day or night. Rather than look to see if it was dark outside men of money (I'm sorry, but women wouldn't be so stupid) rushed to pay a staggering $300,000 for it! The company's chief executive Yvan Arpa said, 'Anyone can buy a watch that tells time – only a truly discerning customer can buy one that doesn't.' Made out of salvage steel from the *Titanic*, the Day & Night watch is a testament to the power of scarcity. The prospect of missing out on such a 'useful' item was too much for some people and it sold out within two days!

Fear is a powerful motivator but it can backfire if you don't understand approach/avoidance. Not to be confused with positive/negative, nor with optimism/pessimism, it simply refers to whether or not someone is motivated towards a goal or away from a problem. You can usually tell which direction someone is by the language they use. For example, someone who is 'approach' may talk about meeting targets or winning new business whereas someone with avoidance tendencies may talk about saving the business or avoiding defeat.

Perhaps it's down to our evolutionary inheritance that we will do more in order to avoid pain than we will do to gain pleasure. Whatever the reason, arousing fear in a prospective client often taps into this instinct and moves them to action.

HERE'S AN IDEA FOR YOU...

Listen out for the verbal clues as to motivational direction and match the style. If your prospect was 'away from' and you talked about all the great benefits they could receive it would fall on deaf ears. To really inspire them to action you should focus on how your product or service could prevent failure. If they are 'towards' motivated, then focus on how your product or service can help them win. Both tap into fear but from a different direction.

18 CREATE CONFIDENCE

Bettger suggests that, 'If you are absolutely sincere, there are many ways you can create confidence with people.' Sincerity is, however, not something you can fake – many have tried and failed miserably. The very best salespeople in the world are sincerely interested in helping the other person ahead of themselves.

DEFINING IDEA...

Confidence awakens confidence.

~ FRIEDRICH III, ELECTOR OF SAXONY

Bettger explains how, in preparation for an interview, 'I imagined myself as a salaried employee... I assumed the role of "assistant buyer in charge of insurance". In this matter my knowledge was superior... Feeling that way, I didn't hesitate to put all the enthusiasm and excitement I could command into what I said. That idea helped me to be absolutely fearless.' The idea of being an assistant buyer in charge of insurance worked so well that Bettger used it from that point on and encouraged young salesmen he met to try the technique, adding 'people don't like to be sold. They like to buy.'

Putting yourself on the side of your prospect creates confidence because you are sincerely attempting to help your client, and not just yourself.

The other way to build confidence, one that is especially powerful in the modern world, is to offer a no-questions-asked guarantee. Business owners and manufacturers often shy away from this idea because of the risk involved. But the bigger risk is not offering a guarantee.

The buying decision is not always an easy one; usually there is no shortage of alternatives about where your prospect could spend money. They don't want to make a mistake or to be made to look foolish, and they certainly don't want to regret their decisions. These issues are, of course, amplified as the 'ticket price' of whatever you are selling increases.

It stands to reason, therefore, that if you can lower the bar and make that decision easier to make then the chances of you gaining a sale are greatly improved. Having a no-strings-attached, 100% money-back guarantee can achieve that.

Apart from making the sale easier and demonstrating to your prospect that you believe in your product or service, a guarantee also taps into the unsung hero of sales and marketing – apathy. You've probably experienced this yourself with cash-back offers on product packaging or money-back guarantees. Even if you are dissatisfied you never quite get around to doing anything about it.

In addition, guarantees help your product or service stand out. If you are in the running with another company and they do not offer a guarantee, then you'll have the edge. Guarantees develop confidence because they prove to the customer that you are prepared to put your money where your mouth is. They raise everyone in the business to a higher standard of operation.

HERE'S AN IDEA FOR YOU...

If your company does not offer a guarantee suggest they introduce one – even for a trial period to monitor results. A blanket guarantee is best because you're not necessarily guaranteeing the product but you are guaranteeing that you will refund money if customers are not happy for whatever reason. All it does is remove the risk from the purchase and encourage the prospect to try the product or service.

19 EXPRESS HONEST APPRECIATION

Bettger suggests that, 'Everyone likes to feel important. People are hungry for praise. People are starving for honest appreciation. But we don't have to go overboard. It is much more effective to be conservative with it.' Too much and it comes over as insincere and annoying. Just be honest and specific.

DEFINING IDEA...

If you give appreciation to people, you win their goodwill. But more important than that, practicing this philosophy has made a different person of me.

~ WILLIAM JAMES, AMERICAN PSYCHOLOGIST AND PHILOSOPHER

Bettger tells how he was leaving the office of a young attorney once when he made a remark that caught the man's attention. It had been his first visit and he had failed to interest the attorney in life insurance. As he was leaving he said, 'Mr Barnes, I believe you have a great future ahead of you. I'll never annoy you, but if you don't mind I'm going to keep in touch with you from time to time.' Mr Barnes questioned Bettger because he obviously thought this was 'some cheap flattery'.

Bettger had, however, seen him speak several nights before and was able to praise his presentation and talk honestly about how other people had done the same. Mr Barnes was thrilled! Bettger asks, 'Do men like you to show that you believe in them and expect bigger things of them? If your interest is sincere, I don't know of anything they appreciate more.'

The key to expressing honest appreciation is the honesty part. Plus, as this story illustrates, specifics are important too. Telling someone how fabulous you think they are is just silly unless a) you really mean it and b) you can back it up with some specific examples. If Bettger had not actually seen the attorney speak, then he would have been caught out and made to look stupid when questioned about his flattery.

Expressing honest appreciation is not something many of us are naturally good at. Perhaps it's a stiff-upper-lip British thing – although Bettger was talking about the United States, so perhaps it's a universal thing!

Perhaps we should all try and give each other a little more appreciation for the things we do. Praise our children more often and expect great things from them, for instance. Be careful of the type of praise you give here, however. Studies have shown that if you praise children for their intelligence they begin to believe they are just smart and don't necessarily have to try that hard. If, on the other hand, you praise them for effort they are more likely to maintain that effort and go on to improve their performance. The key is to be specific with feedback and praise.

Later in his book Bettger says, 'We hear a lot about the starving people of Europe and China, but there are millions of people starving right here in America. Thousands of people right in your city and my city are hungry – hungry for honest praise and appreciation!'

HERE'S AN IDEA FOR YOU...

Next time you think something complimentary about someone, tell them. If you think your partner looks attractive or your daughter has cleaned her room well, then share your praise. Give five genuine compliments every day for a week – but be sure to mean it. If you don't think anything nice then you've got other problems!

20 ASSUME A CLOSE

One of Bettger's most successful sales was made by making a health-check appointment for his prospective client before he sold the policy. It was a bold move but one that set his mind on a successful outcome. He expected to make the sale, and so he made the sale.

We don't get what we want and we rarely get what we deserve – but we do get what we expect!

It was sociologist Robert K. Merton who first coined the phrase 'self-fulfilling prophecy'. In his book *Social Theory and Social Structure* he states, 'The self-fulfilling prophecy is, in the beginning a false definite of the situation evoking a new behaviour which makes the original false conception come "true". This specious validity of the self-fulfilling prophecy perpetuates a reign of error. For the prophet will cite the actual course of events as proof that he was right from the very beginning.'

DEFINING IDEA...
Life is largely a matter of expectation.
– HORACE

Or, to put it another way, if we believe that the outcome will be poor and that we won't make the sale then our actions and behaviours will bring about the result we expect. Say, for example, that you have a meeting with a VIP executive and you are quite nervous. You haven't had much experience in high-end selling, and so you may convince yourself that it is going to be a disaster. Consequently you go to the meeting without the proper preparation because 'it's not going to make any difference anyway'. You lack confidence and make a poor presentation. Needless to say, you don't get the order and tell yourself as you leave, 'See, I knew I was never going to get a result!'

We will rise or fall to meet the expectations both we and others hold about ourselves. This ability to perform to expectation is known as the 'Pygmalion Effect'. It is named after George Bernard Shaw's play *Pygmalion* – probably most widely known in the film musical *My Fair Lady* – in which a professor makes a bet that he can teach a poor flower girl to behave like an aristocrat. The same basic plot idea was used in the 1983 film *Trading Places* with Eddie Murphy and Dan Aykroyd. The Pygmalion Effect is what creates those self-fulfilling prophecies. If you think you won't win the sale then you won't win the sale, because that expectation and attitude will negatively influence your actions and behaviours so that you don't win the sale. Conversely, if you think you will win the sale then your actions, behaviour and attitude will positively influence the outcome in favour of success.

A positive expectation will not always guarantee success – but a negative expectation will always guarantee failure. So take Bettger's advice and 'have a winning attitude'.

HERE'S AN IDEA FOR YOU...

Take a moment to look back on three sales where you won the business and three where you did not. What was your frame of mind at the time? What was also going on in your life at the time? Is there a correlation between the success of the outcome and the attitude you went into the meeting with? If there is, then adopt a winning attitude and assume the close.

21 PUT YOU IN THE INTERVIEW

The final element of successful selling, according to Bettger, is putting the other person into the selling process. In other words, make sure you talk about 'you' and 'yours' instead of 'me' or 'I'. People want to know what you are going to do for them – not the other way around.

DEFINING IDEA...

A man's interest in the world is only an overflow from his interest in himself.
~ GEORGE BERNARD SHAW

Bettger says, 'Years after I began to learn more about basic principles, I analyzed this sale and was surprised to find that I had used the word 'you' or 'yours' sixty-nine times in the short fifteen-minute interview.'

This advice is just as relevant in written communication as it is in face-to-face or other verbal situations, such as phone calls. In business there is a tendency for written communication to be in the third person, and this allows the writer to avoid taking responsibility.

This style of writing may abdicate responsibility but it won't sell squat. Often in business we seem to forget that we are communicating with people and not with machines. Trying to impress people with jargon or corporate language is counterproductive. William Zinsser, author of *On Writing Well*, uses a famous verse from Ecclesiastes and a translation into 'business speak' by the great writer George Orwell to demonstrate how dull this type of communication really is.

Here's the Ecclesiastes:
'I returned and saw under the sun, that the race is not to the swift, nor

the battle to the strong, neither yet bread to the wise, nor riches to men of understanding, nor yet favour to men of skill; but time and chance happeneth to them all.'

Now for Orwell's version:

'Objective consideration of contemporary phenomena compels the conclusion that success or failure in competitive activities exhibits no tendency to be commensurate with innate capacity, but that a considerable element of the unpredictable must invariably be taken into account.'

Zinsser comments, 'Gone from the second one are the short words and vivid images from everyday life – the race and the battle, the bread and the riches – and in their place have waddled the long and flabby nouns of generalised meaning. Gone is any sense if what one person did ("I returned") or what he realised ("saw") about one of life's central mysteries: the capriciousness of fate.'

If you want to engage others and inspire them to action, then don't talk about 'us', 'we', 'I', or disappear behind jargon and corporate-speak. Put the other person into the communication and make it appeal to their hopes and dreams.

Bettger ends by saying, 'I don't remember where I first heard of this test, but it is a superb way for you to make certain you are practicing the most important rule of all: See things from the other person's point of view and talk in terms of his wants, needs, desires.'

HERE'S AN IDEA FOR YOU...

Bettger suggests that you write out what you said in your last sales interview. Count how many times you referred to the other person and how many times you referred to yourself or your organisation. Then see how many places you can find to strike out the personal pronoun ('I' or 'we') and change it to 'you' or 'your'. Put you in your next selling situation.

22 SET GOALS

Bettger says, 'A new idea sometimes produces rapid and revolutionary changes in a man's thinking. For instance, I set a goal for myself to become a "quarter-million-dollar-a-year producer".' Bettger thought that by hard, consistent work, he could make that amount. Having set the goal, he soon produced a quarter million in one day!

Most people, especially those in sales, have heard about the importance of goals and targets. So much so that familiarity has bred contempt and you're likely to have dismissed it as old hat or new-age mumbo-jumbo.

But there is science behind why goal setting is so important. In his brilliant book *The Biology of Belief* Bruce Lipton states, 'When it comes to sheer neurological processing abilities, the subconscious mind is millions of times more powerful than the conscious mind.'

DEFINING IDEA...

Setting goals is the first step in turning the invisible into the visible.

– ANTHONY ROBBINS

His example of how much the subconscious is processing is this: 'if a ball comes near your eye, the slower conscious mind may not have time to be aware of the threatening projectile. Yet the subconscious mind, which processes some 20,000,000 environmental stimuli per second versus 40 environmental stimuli interpreted by the conscious mind in the same second, will cause the eye to blink.'

The difference in 'awareness' between the conscious and subconscious mind is enormous – which effectively means we are unaware of the vast amount of data in the environment that could be of benefit to us.

The big question, therefore, is who decides what we become aware of, and that's why goal setting is so important. If you consciously choose your goals, you instruct a part of the brain responsible for filtration called the reticular activating system (RAS) to look out for anything that could relate to that goal. By doing so, you may become aware of opportunities and ideas that you would not have previously considered before you had a goal.

You will have noticed this in action in your life already. I bought a Border terrier puppy, Bronte, recently and now I see them everywhere. There hasn't been a sudden explosion of Border terriers in my local area. It's just that my RAS now knows I'm interested in Border terriers and is making me aware of them, where I wasn't before we got Bronte.

One of the most popular goal setting techniques is the SMART technique. Your goals should be:
- S – Specific (be precise about what you want to achieve).
- M – Measurable (quantify the goal in some way so you can measure it).
- A – As if Now (write the goal down in the present tense).
- R – Realistic (make the goal possible – it can be a stretch but it has to be possible).
- T – Time specific (put a date on the goal).

Creating the goal allowed Bettger to see and act on opportunities.

HERE'S AN IDEA FOR YOU...

Visualisation and mental rehearsal are an important part of goal setting. You need to visualise yourself having fulfilled your goal. Make sure it is as inspiring as possible and fully engage with the image in your mind. Inject as much emotion into your visualisation as possible as this is what will impact on your subconscious mind. Repeat the mental rehearsal at least twice a day.

23 DON'T ARGUE

Bettger was 'surprised to learn that, as a young man [Benjamin] Franklin couldn't get along with people and made enemies because he argued, made so many positive statements and tried to dominate people'. Winning an argument is almost certainly a guaranteed way to lose a sale.

In Franklin's case, he realised that this confrontational approach wasn't helpful. In an effort to fix his failing he studied Socrates – the Greek philosopher and dramatist who lived in Athens about 2200 years before Franklin was born. Franklin took great delight in developing the Socratic Method of questioning and practised it continually.

DEFINING IDEA...

We must not contradict, but instruct him that contradicts us; for a madman is not cured by another running mad also.
~ ANTISTHENES, GREEK PHILOSOPHER

The Socratic Method is a form of enquiry and debate between people with opposing viewpoints which is based on asking and answering questions to stimulate rational thinking and encourage alternative perspectives. The idea is quite simple, in that if you ask a question or series of questions with which your prospect can readily agree and then ask a concluding question based on those agreements you will end up with a positive response. It is just a way of bringing someone around to your way of thinking without arguing.

Social psychologist Robert B. Cialdini refers to liking as one of the most powerful influencers in human psychology. We are more greatly influenced by people we like and respect. There is nothing mysterious about this – it's just human nature. People do business with people they like. No one likes to be wrong or be made to feel stupid, so battling with someone to prove a point is never going to work as a sales strategy.

So the next time you are in a sales meeting and your prospective client disagrees with you or challenges your opinion, think of the wisdom of Benjamin Franklin: 'When another asserted something that I thought in error, I denied myself the pleasure of contradicting him abruptly, and of showing immediately some absurdity in his propositions.'

Bettger reminds us that, 'We all hate to be outsmarted, outwitted, interrupted or cut off before we finish, by some flannelmouth who knows what we are going to say before we say it. You know the kind; he throws his mouth into high gear before his brain is turning over, explains to you where and why you are mistaken, and straightens you out before you can make yourself clear. By that time, you feel like straightening him out – with a left and right uppercut to the chin! Even if he is right… you'll go two miles out your way to buy the same thing even if you have to pay more.' Remember that no one likes a smart-arse. People would rather have good quality and a great working relationship with someone they like than superior quality and someone they dislike.

HERE'S AN IDEA FOR YOU...

Next time you are going into a sales interview or any conversation where you feel that you are right, don't argue. Instead of making positive statements of your opinion rephrase the statements into questions. Add '…don't you think?' to your statement and make it into a question. That way you still get your point across and can pay the other person the compliment of asking their opinion at the same time.

24 THE IMPORTANCE OF 'WHY?'

According to Bettger, the late Milton S. Hershey, who used to have a candy pushcart and later made millions out of chocolate bars, thought 'why' was so important that he dedicated his life to it!

Our reluctance to assess mistakes is a critical flaw in success in any undertaking. Hershey had three failures before he was forty. He was curious about why that was and put himself through a long quiz. He narrowed the answer down to one reason, which was that he was going ahead without having all the facts.

DEFINING IDEA...

For true success ask yourself these four questions: Why? Why not? Why not me? Why not now?

~ JAMES ALLEN, PHILOSOPHER AND WRITER

In modern times Ricardo Semler, the sometime CEO of Brazilian company Semco, has embraced this philosophy whole-heartedly. When Ricardo joined the family business he and his father clashed. In an amazing display of courage his father transferred his shares to his twenty-one year old son and went on holiday. By 6 p.m. the same day Ricardo had fired 60% of Semco's senior management. Since then Semco has turned the traditional business model on its head and become not only a remarkable social experiment but an extraordinary success.

The company has gone from a few hundred employees to over 3000. Despite a fluctuating Brazilian economy, annual revenue grew from $35 million to $160 million in the ten years between 1994 and 2001. So why did it work so well?

Semco has a cardinal strategy that forms the bedrock for all the innovation in the business: ask why. Semler encourages his people to ask why all the time, and to ask it three times in a row. He argues that this philosophy doesn't come naturally to most people. First, it's considered rude to ask too many questions. People don't like to ask questions because that implies they don't know the answers and are in some way ignorant or uninformed. In addition it opens them up to finding out that what they thought they knew isn't correct. As a result, management is usually scared of people who ask questions because doing so can challenge the status quo. But mostly, says Semler in his book *The Seven-Day Weekend*, 'it means putting aside all the rote or pat answers that have resulted from what I call "crystallized" thinking, that state of mind where ideas have so hardened into inflexible and unquestioned concepts that they're no longer of any use.'

Both Hershey and Semler became very wealthy using this philosophy because it gets to the real reason that often lies behind excuses. According to Bettger, 'The late J Pierpont Morgan Sr., one of the shrewdest business men in all history, once said, "A man generally has two reasons for doing a thing – one that sounds good, and the real one."' Asking 'why' several times allows you to uncover the real one.

HERE'S AN IDEA FOR YOU...

Bettger suggests that the best formula for drawing out the real reason is to ask 'why' and then, once the person gives you an answer, ask, 'Is there anything else in addition to that?' The first response is rarely the real one. And don't accept anything as the 'best way' or the 'only way' just because someone tells you it is. Test it out yourself so you can determine the hallmarks of success and improve your sales record.

25 THE POWER OF SILENCE

Bettger believed that the forgotten art in selling was silence, knowing when to shut up and listen and knowing when to use silence to gain attention. He adds, 'There is nothing new about this. Cicero said two thousand years ago, "There is an art in silence, and there is an eloquence in it too".'

DEFINING IDEA...

The Pause; that impressive silence, that eloquent silence, that geometrically progressive silence which often achieved a desired effect where no combination of words, however so felicitous, could accomplish it.

~ MARK TWAIN

There are two sides to the silence coin. On the one hand, Bettger reminds us of 'the importance of being a good listener, showing the other person you are sincerely interested in what he is saying, and giving him all the eager attention and appreciation that he craves and is so hungry for, but seldom gets!'

He suggests that you look straight into the face of the next person who speaks to you with eager, absorbed interest ('even if it's your own wife') and see the magic effect it has both on yourself, and on the one who is doing the talking.

In everyday life we rarely get an opportunity to talk about the things we are interested in the most. Your loved ones have heard it all before and raise an eyebrow every time you mention your pet subject or pretend to listen with the odd, 'uh huh' interjected at appropriate intervals.

People warm to those who express a genuine interest in what they do. This is why asking questions, then closing your own mouth and listening is such a powerful communication tool. For communication to be successful you don't have to talk.

But when you do, what you say needs to be listened to – which brings us to Bettger's second point on silence. He advocates silence when it's clear that what you are saying is making no impression on the other person, going so far as to say, 'Stop right in the middle of a sentence! Sometimes I stop right in the middle of a word.'

According to Bettger people are never offended and regard it as a courtesy. In most cases, people who are not listening to you have something else on their mind. Until you give them an opportunity to say that, or to put it out of their mind and focus on the discussion at hand, they may look as though they are listening but it's actually a waste of time for both of you. Instead just stop the conversation and wait. Wait until the other person breaks the silence. Bettger warns us that this is not for the faint-hearted and that often the silence is uncomfortable, but don't rush to fill it. Stay quiet and wait for the other person to speak. That way you know you have their attention.

Bettger reminds us that, 'All of us would profit by uttering this prayer every morning: "Oh Lord, help me to keep my big mouth shut, until I know what I am talking about… Amen".'

HERE'S AN IDEA FOR YOU...

We have one advantage that Bettger didn't – the Internet. Before you meet your prospect, hop online. You may be surprised to find that they support a particular charity or work with the local Rotary Club. Ask about issues that interest them and wait. By the end of your meeting you will be considered a great listener and a fascinating person. Instead of thinking what you're going to say next, just listen.

26 HONESTY REALLY IS THE BEST POLICY

Bettger tells a story about a policy he sold with his mentor Karl Collings. The client's health check required a modified policy. Frank pleaded with his colleague, 'Must we tell him, he won't know it, unless you tell him, will he?' 'No,' said Collings quietly, 'but I'll know it. And you'll know it.'

DEFINING IDEA...

I favour any salesman who is absolutely honest about his goods, and who sees their limitations as well as their virtues. I have never had a misunderstanding with such a man.

~ FRANK TAYLOR, ONE-TIME PURCHASING AGENT FOR GENERAL MOTORS

The two of them went back to the client and simply explained the situation clearly. Collings began, 'I could tell you this policy is standard and you probably would never know the difference, but it's not.' He then went on to explain what that meant and, 'without the slightest hesitation', the prospective client took the policy.

Bettger says that watching Karl Collings on that day made him realise why people trusted him. Apart from the fact that he was honest and upfront, Collings turned the challenge in his favour by making the client realise that he could have pulled the wool over his eyes but had chosen not to do so. People respect the truth – even when it's not what they really want to hear.

It took me a while to learn this lesson myself. As a self-employed writer I got it into my head that I really ought to accept every job that came my way. After all, I didn't know when the next one would come along. So whenever I was asked to write something, from a marketing brochure to a book to a website, I would accept the work. This meant that I was often overbooked, something which took a toll on my life. I was working very long hours and never saw my family and friends. Although I would invariably deliver, there were times when I let people down. I soon realised that honesty right from the start is a far smarter and healthier way to live.

Nowadays I just tell people my schedule and more often than not they are happy to wait; if they are not, then I will refer them elsewhere so they can find a suitable alternative. Now I'm booked months in advance and I'm not lying awake at night stressing about getting the jobs done or letting people down. And the added benefit is that my schedule is much more consistent and planned.

If Bettger had sold the modified policy without telling his client the truth it might well never have come to light – but imagine the fireworks if it had. These little choices chip away at our self-esteem and can badly damage a reputation and career.

Bettger closes by saying 'my greatest source of courage, whenever things have looked dark, has come from believing in the wisdom of this philosophy: Not – will the other person believe it. The real test is, do you believe it?'

HERE'S AN IDEA FOR YOU...

Manage people's expectations. Tell prospects the truth about what you can deliver and, where necessary, draw their attention to any potential challenges so they can make choices with their eyes wide open. Turn the challenges into advantages that demonstrate your commitment to full disclosure and integrity. Genuine errors don't usually annoy people; lack of communication about the facts does.

27 ADMIT YOUR FAULTS

Bettger quotes from George Matthew Adams who said 'the wisest and best salesman is always the one who bluntly tells the truth about his article… And if he does not sell the first time, he leaves a trail of trust behind him.' Admitting your faults can achieve this.

DEFINING IDEA...

We only confess our little faults to persuade people that we have no big ones.

~ FRANCOIS, DUC DE LA ROCHEFOUCAULD, FRENCH WRITER

I had a request recently to write a number of training manuals for a business owner in the US. There was a significant amount of work involved and it was very much in my writing domain – business, non-fiction – but I was already committed to other projects, including this one. I wouldn't have been able to start his work for four or five months. Even though I couldn't do the work because of his deadline, I offered to chat to him about it. I called him in the US and we talked for over an hour about the writing, production and publishing side of his requirements. There was no benefit to me for doing this, but in helping him I was able to leave a trail of trust behind me. He was thrilled and I was happy talking about a subject I love.

Being honest at the start, even if that rules you out of the running, is a far better way to operate than trying to pull the wool over someone's eyes. Plus, it's worth noting that admitting faults or challenges can actually have a positive influence on buying behaviour.

In their book *Yes! 50 Secrets from the Science of Persuasion* authors Noah Goldstein, Steve Martin and Robert Cialdini look at some of the quirks of influence. For example, when Doyle Dane Bernbach was asked to introduce a tiny German car into the US market it was an almost insurmountable task. Rather than focus on the strength of the VW Beetle they instead drew attention to its weakness.

Advertising strap lines featuring in the series of ads included slogans such as 'Ugly is only skin deep' and 'It will stay uglier longer'. VW Beetle sales went through the roof. According to the authors of the book 'mentioning a small drawback of a product creates the perception that the company advertising the product is honest and trustworthy. That puts the company in a position to be more persuasive when promoting the product's genuine strengths.' In the Beetle's case it was much more affordable than the US equivalent, and with modest fuel consumption in comparison.

However, Adams reminds us that, 'A customer, as a rule, cannot be fooled a second time by some shady or clever talk that does not square with the truth. Not the best talker wins the sale – but the most honest talker.' Such a person deserves trust which is, according to Bettger, the first rule of successful sales.

HERE'S AN IDEA FOR YOU...

Take a moment to write down all your product or service's weaknesses. Rank them in order of importance and consider how any of them could be viewed in a different light. You will always be able to find a benefit in every challenge; for example, if your restaurant is small, position it as cosy and intimate. Admitting little faults and spinning disadvantages builds trust – essential for sales.

28 KNOW YOUR BUSINESS

Bettger quotes a guy called Billy Rose who wrote a column called 'Pitching Horseshoes'. In it he said, 'This is the age of the specialist. Charm and good manners are worth up to $30 a week. After that, the pay-off is in direct ratio to the amount of specialized know-how in a fellow's head.'

DEFINING IDEA...

There is no substitute for accurate knowledge. Know yourself, know your business, know your men.

~ RANDALL JACOBS, BUSINESSMEN

Bettger tells the story of working out of an office in Philadelphia with sixteen salesmen – but just two of them produced 70% of the business. He noticed that these two were continually being consulted by the other salesmen and finally realised that there was a tangible connection between their performance and the fact that they were so well informed. So he asked one of them where he got all his information. 'I subscribe to services that give all the legal answers, sales ideas, etc., and I read the best journals and magazines,' came the reply.

Knowing your business is not just about knowing your product or service and the features and benefits it offers, it's also about knowing your industry all the way up and down the supply chain. It's not good enough to leave school or university and consider that your education is complete. Where would the world be if we thought we knew all there was to know?

In 1899 Charles H. Duell, commissioner of the US Office of Patents, said, 'Everything that can be invented has been invented.' The chairman of the physics department at Harvard University warned students in 1893 that there was no need for new PhDs in physics. He believed that science had established that the universe was a 'matter machine' that fully obeyed the laws of Newtonian mechanics. That idea has long since been blown out of the water by quantum mechanics.

Leaders are men and woman who know their business. They will make the time to stay informed and continue learning throughout their career. Those who don't are left behind, and give excuses about not having had the time or not having been able to afford it.

Bettger ends, 'If you want to have confidence in yourself, and win and hold the confidence of others, find it an essential rule to: "Know your business and keep on knowing your business".'

And in case you are thinking that you can't teach an old dog new tricks, modern understanding of neuroscience says that you can. In his book *A User's Guide to the Brain* John Ratey says, 'For decades scientists maintained that once its physical connections were completed during childhood, the brain was hard-wired. The tiny neurons and their interconnections were fixed; any neuron or link could die, but none could grow stronger, reorganise or regenerate.' Thanks to imaging technology and clinical research, that is now understood to be false. Learning modifies, strengthens and possibly even re-grows those connections.

HERE'S AN IDEA FOR YOU...

Find out what the best industry magazine or journal in your field is and subscribe to it. If the industry magazines are expensive consider creating a learning group where a few of you share the cost and rotate the reading material. Plus it will help recall and memory if you have someone to discuss it with. The Internet is also a great source of new information in your field.

29 PRAISE YOUR COMPETITORS

One of the best ways to win the confidence of others is to praise your competitors. Most people assume that, when given the chance, you will bash your opponents in an attempt to make your own offering more attractive – but it's never a wise strategy. Praise your competitors instead.

Bettger tells the story of how he went to a meeting where his client told him proudly of the companies he was already insured with. Instead of picking faults with these companies, Bettger replied, 'Well, you've picked the best!'

His prospect was obviously pleased. Bettger then went on to tell him some facts about the companies that he didn't know. And this is why it's so vital to know your business as a whole – knowing about your competitors is also important.

DEFINING IDEA...

I do not speak of what I cannot praise.

~ GOETHE

Far from being bored by this, the additional information made Bettger's prospect feel even better about his decision to insure with those companies. The assumption was that he was 'right' – and we all like to be right! Because Bettger then went on to place his own organisation in the same league as the ones the prospect was familiar with, the man was more prepared to accept Bettger's statements as true. Bettger left with additional business and went on to secure even more, and none of that would have happened had he not praised his competitors.

At the time of writing this book, Ruth Padel, who was elected as Oxford University's Professor of Poetry, had to step down because she criticized her competition. She sent unflattering emails to journalist friends discussing the front-runner for the prestigious post, Derek Walcott. Padel, who was due to succeed Christopher Ricks on 1 October 2009 and become the first woman to hold the post in its 301-year history, had to relinquish the role just nine days after being elected. She acknowledged that sending the emails was 'naive and silly'. As well as losing the obviously much-coveted position, she ended up looking foolish – and acts as a reminder of the validity of Bettger's advice.

In a competitive situation it's never wise to bad-mouth your opposition. Plus, praising your competition is not what people expect, so it can take the fight out of them. They expect you to tell them what's wrong with those companies and why you are better, so when you do the opposite people tend to soften and are more prepared to listen to what you have to say.

Bettger finished the point by quoting from Benjamin Franklin who said, 'I will speak ill of no man – and speak all the good I know of everybody.' Bettger believed this to be rule three of successful selling, and it's one worth remembering in all walks of life.

HERE'S AN IDEA FOR YOU...

In order to praise your competitors you have to know who they are. Take the time to work out who your competition is both nationally and locally. Research those companies to find out more about them – their strengths and weaknesses. Giving unspecific praise is meaningless and will look trite; as such it's likely to end up being counterproductive. Instead find out five key facts about your competitors that you can use in the future.

30 DON'T EXAGGERATE YOUR OFFERING

Bettger tells of how he 'exaggerated the possibilities' of what he was selling. 'It really was misrepresentation,' he confesses. He got rumbled and confides, 'I lost the business; I lost the confidence and respect of my good friend; I lost the respect of my competitor; and worst of all, I lost my own self-respect.'

The natural inclination is to do whatever it takes to get the sale. Sometimes that involves exaggerating the advantages or saying that something is ready when it's not.

This is an age-old argument between sales and development, where salespeople will be out in the field promising all sorts of products and services that are either not possible or have not yet been developed. The temptation to exaggerate is sometimes overwhelming – but it is never wise.

DEFINING IDEA...

To exaggerate is to weaken.

~ JEAN-FRANÇOIS DE LA HARPE, FRENCH PLAYWRIGHT

This failing also happens in marketing where the business owner wants to appeal to the broadest possible target market. The conventional wisdom is that if you do that then you only need a little slice of a big pie to have made your money. It's a false philosophy and one that has seen millions of marketing dollars frittered away on meaningless advertising. Be specific and appeal to your niche.

I remember one client I worked with who wanted a book on property investing. He was a great guy and really passionate about his message. He was totally convinced that property held the key to wealth and that his strategy could help anyone become rich.

DON'T EXAGGERATE YOUR OFFERING

I read what he had written and had him explain the strategy to me so I could get a better understanding of how it all worked. It was crystal clear from that discussion that the strategy would only actually work if the client already had money. It was essentially a strategy for those who had spare cash to invest right now, people who could afford to put large deposits down. It was clever – don't get me wrong – and I could see how it would work, but to say it could help everyone was a gross exaggeration. In the end I convinced him to appeal to his target market and be precise about who he talked to. Yes, he radically reduced his audience but isn't it better to be upfront from the start rather than get tyre-kickers in who are not in a position to take advantage of the advice? Far better to go for a larger slice of a much smaller pie!

Bettger warns, 'It was a bitter experience. I was so shocked at my blunder that I thought of it all that night. I was years recovering from the humiliation of it.' He made up his mind to never again want anything he was not entitled to – because it costs too much!

HERE'S AN IDEA FOR YOU...

Who is your target market? Right now, who is perfectly placed for the product or service you offer in its current form? Make a list of your favourite clients and work out if they share any common characteristics. If they do, then go after other people like them rather than trying to convince someone who is not suited to your offering that it can be adapted or altered in some way.

31 FIND RELIABLE WITNESSES

Bettger uses the analogy of a trial lawyer in demonstrating the power of reliable expert witnesses and suggests that the same is true of successful sales. He says, 'A good testimony from a reliable witness exerts a powerful influence on the court.'

DEFINING IDEA...

If you do build a great experience, customers tell each other about that. Word of mouth is very powerful.

~ JEFF BEZOS, FOUNDER OF AMAZON

You may remember I referred to the work of social psychologist Robert B. Cialdini earlier. So far I have mentioned two of his six psychological principles that direct human behaviour – scarcity and liking. Finding reliable witnesses taps into a further two of those principles – authority and social proof.

We are innately influenced by authority figures. If you are unsure how accurate this is, then consider the influence a doctor wields in his or her crisp white coat. We generally believe what the doctor tells us so completely and without question that the belief alone can help or hinder healing. It is this principle which is partly responsible for the power of placebo medicine. We have a deep-seated sense of duty to authority.

The other principle is social proof. This says that, 'We view a behaviour as correct in a given situation to the degree that we see others performing it.' Social proof is especially relevant when we are deciding on a particular course of action or are in unfamiliar situations. Here we will instinctively look to others to see what they are doing as a way of deciding what we should be doing ourselves.

The reason all this is relevant to selling is that Bettger talked about the impact of having an expert witness – someone who could vouch for the effectiveness or quality of your product. This can be seen in the power of word-of-mouth advertising. There is nothing more compelling than an endorsement from someone you know. As a result, Bettger asked people he worked with for referrals and used those as an introduction to get an appointment with a prospect.

Bettger would call up the person who'd given him the referral when in a meeting with the relevant prospect, and pass them over to his prospect so the two could confer. The prospect would ask questions and be assured of the value of the offering because they already knew the person they were talking to. This is social proof and authority in action. And it's a powerful way to sell. Nowadays it may not be possible to do what Bettger did because you rarely get through to a real person on the phone any more, but it is possible to carry testimonials from happy clients or people in perceived positions of authority. These will carry weight and help the prospect make the buying decision.

Bettger says that, 'An infallible way to gain a man's confidence quickly is to "Bring on your Witness".'

HERE'S AN IDEA FOR YOU...

Every time you have a happy client, and they tell you about how great your product or service is, ask if you can quote them. Gathering written testimonials doesn't have to be a laborious task. Just make a note of what was said and email the person to ensure you got their words down correctly, and then get permission to use it in your sales and marketing.

32 DRESS TO IMPRESS

Someone once said, 'Clothes don't make the man, but they do make 90% of what you see of him.' Unless you look the part, people won't believe what you say is important. They will make an assumption about your ability to help them within seconds of your first meeting.

The truth of this is brilliantly demonstrated by the UK TV programme called *The Real Hustle*. The show alerts its viewers to many common confidence tricks that are being used up and down the country in an attempt to demonstrate just how gullible we all are and hopefully stop a few people falling for cons. The number of times that the con involves a fake security guard or policeman is amazing!

DEFINING IDEA...

You never get a second chance to make a first impression.

~ PROVERB

In one example a man posing as a security guard offered to take the coats of patrons in a trendy bar. The rouse was that there had been a few thefts in the area so they were putting the valuables away in a cloakroom. Without exception, the customers handed over their possessions. All this happened without the bar owner's knowledge, so all hell broke loose when the customers later went to collect their things and discovered they were missing. Obviously all the people affected got their things back, but they were astonished at how easily they had jumped to conclusions and handed everything over. Such is the power of looking the part!

If the right clothes can make usually sensible people part with their belongings then surely looking the part is important in business.

Bettger finally learned this lesson when an old fellow he refers to as a 'forty-minute egg' sat him down with some good advice. 'You let your hair grow so long you look like an old-time football player... You don't know how to tie your tie... And your color combinations are positively funny!'

He was advised to put himself in the hands of an expert. This is solid advice, even now – especially if you have the fashion sense and colour co-ordination ability of a newt! In Bettger's case, he was advised to save up for one really good suit rather than trying to economise. In addition, he found a good barber and made a standing appointment so that he always looked neat and presentable.

We might not like the idea that we are judged by everything from the cut of our hair to the cut of our suit, but get over it. It's the same for everyone, male or female, so if you want to be successful in sales – or in anything else for that matter – make an effort with your appearance.

Bettger says, 'When you feel well dressed, it improves your mental attitude towards yourself, and gives you more self-confidence.' Always look your best so you put your best foot forward.

HERE'S AN IDEA FOR YOU...

Bettger's advice, straight from his tailor, is 'that after each wearing, your coat and vest should be hung on a hanger and your trousers hung straight, not over the hanger's crossbar. If you do this, the creases will disappear and clothes will rarely need pressing, until you send them to a dry cleaner.'

33 SMILE!

Bettger admits, 'As a young man I had the major handicap that would have meant sure failure if I hadn't found a way to correct it quickly. I had the sourest puss you ever gazed on in all your life.' The inability to smile is a major handicap – especially in sales.

Bettger apparently didn't have an easy life; his father died when he was a boy, leaving his mother with five small children and no insurance. It was the time known as the 'Gay Nineties' although they weren't very gay for them!

When he entered the world of selling many years later he discovered that a 'sour puss' brought consistent results: 'an unwelcome audience and failure'.

DEFINING IDEA...
Life is like a mirror. Smile at it and it smiles back at you.
~ PEACE PILGRIM, AMERICAN PACIFIST

I'm sure you've had the experience where you've been in a shop or in a buying situation and the sales person is smiling while every fibre of their body is screaming 'It's late, hurry up, I'm going out tonight!' This person might be beaming from ear to ear because some sales training course told them it was conducive to selling, but what about the cacophony of contradictory messages we receive through body language? You can even pick up the contradiction on the phone: think of telesales staff who obviously have laminated notices in their booths that encourage them to smile before making that call.

So, are all smiles equal?

Social scientist Alicia Grandey and her colleagues say 'no' . They wanted to know if there was a difference in effectiveness depending on the type of smile. Based on previous findings demonstrating that people can often distinguish between authentic and inauthentic smiles, they wanted to see if smiling affected customer satisfaction.

In one study participants watched several videos of conversations between a hotel employee and a guest where the employee was to perform a task. The script was always the same but the employee behaved slightly differently. In the first video the employee was asked to generate positive feelings towards the guest and think about how she could make the guest feel good. This was a replication of the authentic approach. In the other example she was told she was required to smile – inauthentic. The employee was then to do a task well and poorly.

Obviously the guest was happier when the task was done well. When it was done poorly, whether the employee was smiling authentically or not made little difference. However, if the task was done well and with an authentic smile, the observers registered a far higher level of customer satisfaction.

Bettger suggests you 'give every living soul you meet the best smile you ever smiled in your life, even your own wife and children, and see how much better you feel and look. It's one of the best ways I know to stop worrying and start living.'

HERE'S AN IDEA FOR YOU...

Telling someone to create an authentic smile is an oxymoron – if it was authentic you wouldn't have to tell them to smile, so this is not as easy as it sounds. A suggestion comes from Benjamin Franklin who said, 'Search others for their virtues.' Instead of finding fault with people you deal with, make a mental list of five attributes you admire. This different perspective will help make your smile authentic.

34 ACTION FOLLOWS FEELING

Bettger worked hard to remove his sour puss and generate a positive attitude. He says his 'experience seems to substantiate the theory of the great philosopher and teacher, Professor William James of Harvard: "Action seems to follow feeling".' What he would do and how successful he would be therefore depended on how he felt.

DEFINING IDEA...

There is nothing either good or bad but thinking makes it so.

~ WILLIAM SHAKESPEARE

If action seems to follow feeling; feeling seems to follow thought. James qualifies his statement by saying, 'But really action and feeling go together; and by regulating the action, which is under the more direct control of the will, we can indirectly regulate the feeling, which is not.' But this is not strictly true. He didn't account for the power of thought and how that can regulate feeling. And as we have direct control over our thoughts and can theoretically change our mind in a heartbeat, then we also have control over emotion through what we focus on and think about.

Just think about it logically for a moment. When you are happy you are usually thinking happy thoughts: a sale has gone well, that positive thought leads to another positive thought and soon you're creating a virtuous circle. You find yourself in situations and with people that make you happy. If, on the other hand, you are down in the dumps – the appointment went badly, the traffic is terrible – you start thinking about negative thoughts: the bills that need to be paid, etc. You create a vicious circle. Both situations started with a thought when you made the situation or event mean something, and got into an emotional rut as a result.

The power of thought is now well documented. There is even a branch of science called epigentics which studies how the body is affected by thought. One of my favourite demonstrations of just how potent it is comes from research done by Cleve Baxter. One day he was isolating white cells so he could study them. To do this he centrifuged his saliva to get a concentrated number of white cells, then placed them in a small test tube and inserted gold wire electrodes connected to EEG-type equipment. He had the sudden idea to make a small cut on the back of his hand to see if this might affect his cells. He searched the lab for a sterile scalpel and came back to the test tube. He glanced at the chart that was recording the electromagnetic activity of the white cells – and it had already registered intense activity. The thought that he would cut his hand was enough for his white cells to react as though he had cut his hand.

Bettger reminds us that emotion is contagious, and if we exude enthusiasm and positivity we are much more likely to receive them in return.

HERE'S AN IDEA FOR YOU...

Make a playlist of the music that reminds you of happy times, or that you love and you can't help dancing to. Whenever you are down, remember that your decision-making process is impaired and force yourself to listen to the playlist. Preferably move around while you are listening so you can break the negative cycle and replace it with happy thoughts.

35 HOW TO REMEMBER NAMES AND FACES

Whatever your profession, remembering names is just common courtesy. Bettger says, 'The first thing that helped me to remember names and faces was to forget myself, and concentrate as hard as I could on the other person, his face, and his name. This helped me overcome self-consciousness when meeting strangers.'

DEFINING IDEA...

Remember that a person's name is to that person the sweetest and most important sound in any language.

~ DALE CARNEGIE

Bettger offers a solution to help remember names and faces: I-R-A (Only in this case no armies, Irish or otherwise, are involved.)

Impression

Apparently, 'psychologists tell us that most of our memory troubles are really not memory troubles at all; they are observation troubles'. Many people may remember the name or the face but never both of them together, usually because they have been drawn to one or the other by some immediate impression – and have forgotten or paid insufficient attention to the other element. If a person's name is unusual they will be preoccupied with that and forget the face, or if they don't catch the name but do remember the face they won't think to ask someone to repeat the name. Bettger notes that if he didn't catch a name he skipped past it – and yet he acknowledged that if someone did the same to him he felt hurt. So he made a real effort to observe a person's face and get a clear, vivid impression of the name.

Repetition

To prevent you forgetting someone's name within minutes of meeting them, Bettger suggests that you 'repeat it several times quickly in your mind. Plus it helps to repeat it out loud too, so you might say, "Nice to meet you, Mr Musgrave".' Then, during the conversation, use this name a few more times to cement it into your memory.

This is the technique used by shop staff to ensure they give the correct change. When you give a note to pay for a purchase, the cashier will generally repeat out loud the denomination of the note you handed over so that they give the correct change. When you are dealing with money all day it would be easy to make a mistake otherwise.

Association

We log memories by association. So connect the name and face to the occasion you met at, associate it with an action picture and if possible include the person's business in the picture. It will then be easier to recall later.

In the film *Erin Brockovich* there's a scene where Erin reels off the names, addresses, telephone numbers and medical conditions of the plaintiffs involved in her case to the snooty female lawyer who is taking it over. She has strong associative memories of those people because she's been so involved.

Bettger also suggests you write down the name and any key points you've learned in the conversation as soon as possible.

HERE'S AN IDEA FOR YOU...

If you have a difficult name or one that is easily spelled or pronounced incorrectly, help other people when you meet. It's embarrassing when you forget someone's name so help others to avoid this embarrassment. Bettger used to help with the pronunciation of his name by saying 'Bet-cher life!' If you have an unusual name, spell it for people or help with the pronunciation. It will be a relief for them and help you stand out.

36 MASTER THE ART OF BREVITY

Apparently one of Bettger's best friends took him aside one day and said, 'Frank, I can't ask you a question without you taking fifteen minutes to answer it, when it should only take one sentence!' We are all different and require information in different ways.

The penny finally dropped when Bettger was interviewing a busy executive who said, 'Come to the point! Never mind all those details.' The executive didn't care about the arithmetic. He just wanted the answer.

DEFINING IDEA...

The most valuable of all talents is that of never using two words when one will do.

~ THOMAS JEFFERSON

The most useful personality profiling tool I've ever come across is Instinctive Drive (ID). As the name would suggest, it is concerned with instinct rather than behaviour and was helpful to me in working out different communication styles. ID exposes your natural operating system and provides a profile of four drives: verify, authenticate, complete and improvise. You can be driven by each, or you can avoid each drive. Knowing my own ID has helped me to a) appreciate my own quirks and learn how to get the best out of myself and b) realise that there are innate differences between people which are not born out of a desire to be deliberately annoying.

For example, my brother and I have very different communication and decision-making styles. My guess is that if he did his ID he would be almost an exact opposite to me. He needs to think about all the issues and turn things over in his head for a while. He thinks through every single option, assesses the risks and then decides. And if I'm on the receiving end of that, or if I need some instructions from him, I find it incredibly frustrating because all I'm interested in is the bottom line. I don't need to hear how he arrived at the conclusion he finally reached; I just need the conclusion. I love him to bits, but seriously I could wring his neck sometimes – and I know the feeling is mutual!

In the end you have to try and match what the other person needs, not what you need. If you are familiar with your client then you may know how that person prefers their information – with brevity or in detail.

If you are visiting someone for the first time then it's best to assume brevity. Cut to the chase but be fully prepared to deliver detail should that be required. Make sure your prospect knows that you are being brief to respect their time, but should they have any questions you have all the information to hand. That way you respect their time without waffling on, but have the additional information if they do want it. Bettger reminds us that, 'A salesman cannot know too much but he can talk too much.'

HERE'S AN IDEA FOR YOU...

Bettger suggests that you '"set off the alarm clock" on yourself. If your listener doesn't insist on your finishing, then you know you've been dragging it out.' Practise your pitch with a number of different lengths so you can best match the communication style of the person you are meeting. Use the alarm-clock technique to monitor when it's time to shut up.

37 ADMIT WHEN YOU'RE SCARED

There came a point in Bettger's sales career when eking out a bare existence wasn't enough. He realised he needed to call on some more important people who would buy larger policies so he could earn bigger commissions. He says, 'Scared is no word for it. I was terrified!'

DEFINING IDEA...

It is a sign of strength, not of weakness, to admit that you don't know all the answers.

~ JOHN P. LOUGBRANE, WRITER

In his first interview with a 'big-shot' he was so nervous that, 'I lost my nerve completely and just couldn't go on.' Shaking with fear and faced with the prospect of a disastrous meeting, Bettger took the unlikely step of admitting how he felt, 'Mr Hughes... I... uh... I've been trying to see you for a long while... and, uh... now that I'm here, I'm so nervous and scared, I can't talk!'

First, his nerves disappeared, and second Mr Hughes noticeably softened. He was obviously pleased to be regarded so highly and said he felt the same way when he was a young man and encouraged Bettger to take his time.

There is an assumption in business that we always have to have the right answers or must appear to have our act together all the time. Admit no weakness, never say sorry, always present a tough exterior no matter what you really feel. And yet Bettger demonstrated heart-on-your-sleeve honesty and it made a real impact.

It also demonstrates that conventional wisdom isn't always correct. I read recently that winning someone over to your way of thinking can often be assisted if you inconvenience them. Again, conventional wisdom would say this was lunacy and yet research says otherwise.

Behavioural researchers Jon Jecker and David Landy demonstrated this in a study where participants won some money from the experimenters in a contest. Afterwards one group of participants was approached by the experimenter who asked if they'd give the money back because he was using his own funds and didn't have any left. Almost all of them agreed. Another group of participants was not approached for the refund. Later all participants were surveyed about how much they liked the experimenter. Jecker and Landy found that those who were inconvenienced and asked for the money back liked the experimenter more than those who got to keep the money!

People usually respond positively towards genuine vulnerability, and they don't mind being inconvenienced if the motive is genuine.

Bettger says 'there is no disgrace in admitting you are scared, but there is a disgrace in failing to try'. I would add to that by saying that there is disgrace in trying to cover up fear or vulnerability with arrogance or bravado. If you mess up, say sorry; if you are scared say so and ask for a moment to compose yourself – and you may be surprised at the results.

HERE'S AN IDEA FOR YOU...

If you fluff a presentation or important meeting – regroup. If you try and force yourself to continue you'll probably make an arse of it anyway, so try a different approach. Apologise to the group and say you are so nervous because it's important that you get this right. Your audience will be flattered that you care so much and will probably soften, and vocalising your feelings helps to disperse them so you can continue.

38 THE SALE BEFORE THE SALE

Bettger tells the story of watching a large ship dock at Miami and how it taught him an important lesson in sales. 'Right there it dawned on me why I had been losing too many promising-looking prospects on my approach. I had been trying to throw them the hawser.'

Initially a small, thin rope with a weighted ball called a 'monkey's fist' is thrown to the shore. This is called a 'heaving line' and is connected to the hawser – a thick, heavy rope which is then wrapped around upright iron posts. The captain told Bettger, 'It would be impossible to throw the hawser far enough over the side of the ship to make connection with the pier.'

It's the same in sales – we try and go for the big sale straight off the bat and it just doesn't connect. Especially when there's no relationship with the person or company involved.

DEFINING IDEA...

Great things often come from small beginnings.

~ FINNISH PROVERB

As a ghost writer, I do a lot of work with international speakers and businesspeople who want to produce a book. Not only does a book give them kudos and turn them into overnight 'experts', but it also acts as a heaving line for additional products and services. The low entry point of a book makes it extremely accessible for most people; they read it, like what they read and often decide to hire the business or attend courses by the speaker – and that's where the real money is.

It is possible, however, to use this idea consciously and it can be a very effective sales technique known as perceptive contrast. I was in Australia in July 2008 with my family and the kids wanted to go on the jet boat ride on Sydney Harbour. This particular jet boat experience was hailed as the fastest on offer and required that participants remove their shoes and sport an attractive full length purple poncho; we were obviously going to get wet. I asked at the kiosk how much it would be for two adults and two children. I can't remember the exact amount, but it was well over $250 dollars – which was met with a sharp intake of breath and mutterings on my part! To cut a long story short, another man then appeared on the desk and suggested that because the boat was nearly full he'd give the tickets to me for about $170. I, of course, accepted and we all got wet.

Whether knowingly or not, the salesman had opened the offer so high that when it was lowered I jumped at the chance. In contrast this seemed like a bargain, even though it was still an expensive way to get drenched!

Unless you are deliberately using perceptual contrast, don't set the bar too high initially.

HERE'S AN IDEA FOR YOU...

Look at every sale as the opening of a relationship rather than a one-off transaction. Introduce your offer and start with a lower-priced product or service so as not to scare prospects off. Once the prospect has bought something, even something small, they are more likely to be upgraded to a bigger purchase. If you are going for the king, hit straight off the bat – one way to ensure you get better results is to guarantee your offering so the customer feels safe in the purchase.

39 BE RESPECTFUL OF THE GATEKEEPERS

According to Bettger 'Many salesmen don't seem to realise that a man's secretary can be so important to them. In many cases, she is the power behind the throne… she frequently is the big shot's boss so far as his time for appointments in concerned.' Don't get on her (or his) wrong side!

First of all, you have to appreciate there are two types of gatekeepers. There are the receptionists who handle all the calls to the organisation and then there are the executive assistants or personal assistants who handle calls to the office of the person you are trying to reach.

DEFINING IDEA...

If you respect others, others will respect you.

~ JAPANESE PROVERB

Anthony Parinello, author of *Selling to VITO – the Very Important Top Officer*, suggests that you should never seek to speak to VITO directly. If you do you will only be met with a barrage of questions designed to get rid of you as fast as possible; the receptionists will be warned not to connect calls willy-nilly. So instead find out who VITO's personal assistant is and seek to be put through to them directly.

If you are seeking to speak to Ms Brown, head of the company, Parinello suggests that when you phone the main switchboard you don't ask to be connected to Ms Brown or to Ms Brown's PA, but that you find out the name of Ms Brown's assistant and say, 'Please can you connect me with Mr White in Ms Brown's office. Thank you.' According to Parinello, who conducted 12,000 interviews with gatekeepers and receptionists, they are rarely in that role through choice; they are cooling their heels until the job they really want comes up. As such, 'Anyone who is in a position of necessity will respond to an implied request much faster than someone who's in that same position by choice.' Adding the thank you at the end is therefore not just courteous but implies that they will take action.

For the record, another finding from those 12,000 interviews was that gatekeepers hate being lied to by salespeople. Saying you are returning a call when you're not or pretending to know someone when you don't is bad form and will not endear you long term – so don't do it.

Of course all this is pointless if you haven't done your research and have spent weeks getting in to see the wrong person. Parinello refers to these people as 'Seymours' – they rarely have the authority to buy and will always want to 'see more'.

Bettger reminds us that, 'A clever man with a dominating personality may often get by the secretary without stating the purpose of his call; a salesman with lots of nerve and a fluent tongue may get away with it once in a while; but I believe the best way to outsmart secretaries and switchboard operators is never to try!' Treat the gatekeeper with the same reverence you would the person you are trying to see.

HERE'S AN IDEA FOR YOU...

If you don't know who the gatekeeper is then find out. Read company information and visit the company website. Look at the corporate information pages or those that tell you about personnel; you may also find newsletters or staff bulletins. If all else fails, call the switchboard to find out and make sure you get the correct spelling and pronunciation. Don't ask to be connected then. Hang up and make the call later.

40 PRACTICE MAKES PERFECT

Again Bettger applied his experience in baseball to selling. His manager, while he was playing for Greenville, told him, 'Frank, if you could hit, the big-league clubs would be after you.' Apparently another player had been no better than Frank but practising made him 'one of the greatest hitters in baseball'.

DEFINING IDEA...

Practice is the best master.

~ LATIN PROVERB

In an effort to improve his hitting he and a fellow player would practise with 300 balls every day and pay local kids a few nickels to return the balls. Both he and his teammate were later sold to the St Louis Cardinals. Ten years later Bettger applied the same principle to selling and practised his presentation until he knew it inside out and back to front. It was the relentless practising that made him successful.

We have a tendency to believe that brilliant people are just talented or that fate dealt them a particularly good hand. What we rarely appreciate is that brilliance is more often than not the result of relentless practising. To be successful in any walk of life you need to master your craft – and that is true of musicians, salespeople or sports stars.

Sir Alex Ferguson once said, 'David Beckham is Britain's finest striker of a football not because of a God-given talent but because he practises with a relentless application that the vast majority of less gifted players wouldn't contemplate.' There are stories of Beckham being pulled off the pitch in the pouring rain as a young lad as he tried to bend the ball. Talent alone is never enough; it is the willingness to practise relentlessly that makes the good great.

And for those who are thinking, 'I don't have the head space for all this practising' – think again. It's been discovered that as you learn a new skill and practise it over and over again the part of your brain related to that particular learning will increase in size. Once you master the skill, however, the area of your brain responsible for the learning shrinks again as the skill transfers from a learned skill to an unconscious competence. It is, in other words, delegated to parts of the brain lower down the chain of command. According to John Ratey, in his book *A User's Guide to the Brain*, 'The expanded portion of the executive part of the brain, the cerebral cortex, was no longer needed to carry out the skill. This commanding part of the brain reverted back to its original size, freeing up neurons to learn other things.'

Bettger reminds us that, 'You can't develop that perfection by looking in the mirror and congratulating your company for taking you on. You've got to drill and drill and drill!' Whatever you are trying to master, you must dedicate time and effort to practising.

HERE'S AN IDEA FOR YOU...

If you are making a presentation, the more you know the material and all the possible objections you could encounter, the more prepared you'll be. The more prepared you are, the more confident you are – regardless of who it is you are meeting. Run through your presentation at least five times a day. Try and find out new and interesting information that can be added to make it more compelling and interesting.

41 DEMONSTRATE YOUR PRODUCT OR SERVICE

According to Bettger, there's an old Chinese proverb that says, 'One demonstration is worth more than a thousand words.' And he goes on to say that a good rule is 'never dramatize anything yourself that you can get the prospect or customer to do'. Actions speak louder than words.

DEFINING IDEA...

A picture is worth a thousand words.

~ PROVERB

The Restaurant is a TV show where couples compete to open a restaurant with legendary chef Raymond Blanc.

Each week one couple is eliminated after completing a challenge. One week the task was to give a cookery demonstration at an assigned location. One couple was given a rowing regatta as their venue and produced what looked like beautiful food but wouldn't let anyone taste it! Their logic was that if the people watching the demonstration liked the look of the food they would book a table for dinner that evening. Guess how many bookings they made? Not one.

Being able to demonstrate what your company offers is a powerful way to sell. It gets people involved and short-cuts the buying cycle, so think of ways in which you can allow your prospective customers to experience for themselves how good it is. If the team who cooked at the regatta had allowed people to taste the food they were offering they would have undoubtedly got bookings for their restaurant. Instead they looked like idiots.

An extension of this idea is reciprocity. Reciprocity is another of the principles that powerfully directs human behaviour, as discussed by Robert B. Cialdini in his book *Influence: Science and Practice*. Basically, if you give somebody something for nothing there is an innate desire to balance the books.

This law of reciprocity is activated when companies give you samples of their product or other gifts. This same law turned the Hare Krishna organisation into a fundraising goldmine. Prior to the 1970s, fundraising efforts had met with mixed results. Then they changed tack and started to give would-be donors a gift of a book or a flower. The receiver of the flower felt an internal compulsion to reciprocate the gift with a donation, and even if they didn't want the flower or tried to return the book they still gave a donation.

Being able to demonstrate your offering or find a way for the prospective client to sample what you have to offer will radically improve your success rate. Bettger suggests that you 'let the customer perform. Put him into action. In other words: Let the customer help you make the sale.' Bettger realised one day that he had bought thirty-three cars in his career and was even more surprised to realise that thirty-three salesmen had sold him those cars. Not one of them had thought it pertinent to stay in touch with him, to form an on-going relationship. As a result they lost numerous sales. This is a problem for most people in sales. If they sell lower-ticket items they often don't think it necessary to maintain contact with past clients, and are so busy trying to find new ones that the ones they have had in the past are ignored. Those who sell high-ticket items assume that there will not be that much repeat purchasing anyway so there isn't much point in maintaining a relationship. And yet, as Bettger demonstrated with his car example, high-ticket items maybe bought far more frequently than you think.

HERE'S AN IDEA FOR YOU...

Think about ways you could use some of the new technology to short-cut the buying cycle. Create a professional video file of your presentation together with a demonstration of how it works. If possible, think of ways to make the presentation interactive. Use YouTube or podcasts to spread your message.

42 NEVER FORGET A CUSTOMER; NEVER LET A CUSTOMER FORGET YOU

Besides, even if the person you sold to only buys once in a blue moon, you can still make it work for you if you treat your customers well and stay in touch with them. Offer them ways to help them get the best out of their purchase and then they will tell others about you should they ever be asked for a referral.

DEFINING IDEA...

You can't buy loyalty, you can only invest in it.

~ RONNY M. COLE, AUTHOR

Bettger also makes a good point in that you should always go out of your way to help every customer, regardless of the size of their purchase – you never know who they are. He tells the story of how a plainly dressed little old lady walked into a department store. The other clerks paid no attention to her but one young clerk waited on her courteously and even carried her bags to her car, protecting her from the rain with his umbrella. A few days later the head of the store received a letter from Andrew Carnegie thanking them for looking after his mother so well and giving them a large order. That sales clerk went on to become the head of a great department store himself. It's a bit like the scene from the film *Pretty Woman* when the Julia Roberts character goes into a upmarket shop in her hooker outfit and is met with scorn and disdain, only to return a day later with Richard Gere and his credit cards.

Regardless of who people are, if you are to ensure that customers never forget you and that you don't forget them, you should treat them all well and do whatever you need to do to ensure they are happy with their purchase and feel fully supported in their buying decision.

Stay in touch and don't ever allow a customer, past or present, to forget who you are.

HERE'S AN IDEA FOR YOU...

Go back to past clients and ask them if there was anything that could have been improved; perhaps the instruction manual could have been clearer or perhaps they would have appreciated a follow-up call to make sure they were OK. Implement the best suggestions and send a thank-you card. The reconnection may inspire a new order; at the very least, they will feel valued at having had their opinion sought.

43 SOURCE NEW LEADS FROM PAST CLIENTS

Having watched Willie Hoppe win the world billiard championship, Bettger realised that selling was just like billiards. 'It is just as important to play position for the next shot in selling, as it is in billiards. In fact it is the lifeblood of our business.' You need to plan for future sales too.

Like billiards, the game of selling is won or lost not by the balls you sink but by your ability to constantly set up the next shot. Making a sale without any regard for how you will make the next sale is short-sighted and foolish. If you can do everything in your power to make sure your prospect is happy then not only will they be more likely to buy from you again – even if the type of purchase isn't that frequent – but they are much more likely to give you leads if you ask for them.

DEFINING IDEA...

In sales, a referral is the key to the door of resistance.

~ BO BENNETT, AUTHOR AND SPEAKER

According to Bettger, 'new customers are the best source of new business'. And he used a novel way of getting his customers to introduce him to their friends and colleagues. He created small cards the size of a modern business card with 'Introducing Franklin L. Bettger' printed on the middle of the card. Above this the customer would write the name of a person he knew personally whom he thought might benefit from Bettger's services. Below this, the customer would sign the card. Frank would then use this card to gain an appointment with his new prospect.

I'm not sure how well that would work now, but the concept is still sound.

The best advertising and marketing you and your business can ever have is 'word of mouth'. Despite all the modern technology and fancy ways for us to communicate with our prospects and clients, an old-fashioned referral is still the most popular way for people to source suppliers.

In a RainToday.com and Wellesley Hill Group research report, *How Clients Buy: A Benchmark Report on Marketing and Selling Professional Services from the Client Perspective*, buyers of professional services were asked how they went about finding providers. Predictably the top method of finding providers was referrals. And this is despite all the expensive advertising and marketing gimmicks that exist today.

The problem with referrals is that we tend to assume that if our clients are happy they will naturally tell people about us anyway, so we don't actually have to ask. That's a mistake. If you piss your customer off they will shout about you from the rooftops; if you do a good job they probably won't mention it to anyone – even if you wow them. That is, unless you go out of your way to ask them to.

Bettger reminds us that 'if you take care of your customers, they'll take care of you'.

HERE'S AN IDEA FOR YOU...

Bettger suggests that if you do get a lead you should follow it up immediately. Regardless of the outcome, go back to your customer and tell them what happened and show your appreciation for the lead they gave you. That way they feel valued and informed, plus if it doesn't work out they may even give you an alternative lead. Always treat your lead with the utmost respect and attention, otherwise it reflects badly on you and potentially on your customer.

44 APPEAL FOR ACTION

Bettger talks of the seven rules in closing a sale. The first is saving the closing points for the close. Don't use the closing points too early. Apparently 'the average successful sale goes through four steps: Attention, Interest, Desire and Close'. The close must call for action.

DEFINING IDEA...

You never asked me.

- HENRY FORD

when asked by an insurance agent whom he had known for many years why he never got any of Ford's business.

One of the fundamental mistakes that most salespeople make is to stop at step three. They successfully grab the attention and generate some interest in the offer, so the prospective customer desires the product or service. Then they just fail to ask for the order.

You can't assume that if you do the first three it's a natural hop to the close. It's not.

Apathy is a wonderful thing if you have signed someone up to a membership deal which will pay you revenue for years to come. Even if they want to cancel the membership it will take them years to 'get around to it'. If, on the other hand, you want people to take action, then apathy will almost certainly work against you. You have to ask for the order or call them to action in some way – otherwise they just won't get around to it.

It sounds obvious, but the call to action is the thing that is most often missed in sales or advertising messages. I remember seeing a great ad poster campaign for guide dogs. It really was a brilliant ad, only there was no call to action anywhere on this enormous poster. No phone number, no website, no ask of any sort whatsoever. I emailed the company because I was so surprised and asked them why they had done it that way. The response was that it was a 'brand-awareness campaign'. Personally I think that's a synonym for a sales campaign that was either cocked up in some way or just didn't work.

Why on earth would anyone spend thousands creating a billboard when they could also have asked for donations or support in some way?

Bettger's idea probably came from the American advertising and sales pioneer St Elmo Lewis. In 1898 Lewis developed a practical sales tool using the latest scientific management insights of the time. He created his AIDA funnel model on customer studies in the US life insurance market to explain the stages of selling, and that's probably where Bettger came across it. Lewis maintained that the most successful salespeople led people through a four-stage process when convincing prospective clients of a new idea or new product: awareness, interest, desire and, finally, action. He believed that if you did the first three hierarchical stages properly then action was a natural result. But it pays to be sure.

Bettger obviously agreed, and today the AIDA model is still alive and well and is recognised by sales and marketing professionals around the world.

HERE'S AN IDEA FOR YOU...

Take a moment to think of the last five sales situations that you were involved in which didn't work out. Did you ask for the sale or were you too busy explaining the benefits or talking about other issues? Never, ever forget to ask for the sale.

45 GATHER MOMENTUM

The remaining six rules of closing are all about getting momentum towards a yes. The close is all about summarising effectively and finding ways to get your prospective client to agree with you at intervals towards the close. This builds a positive momentum which will help your prospective client say the final 'yes'.

Bettger's second rule is to be able to summarise the most compelling aspects of your presentation. He tells of one great sales manager who used to insist that his salesman could 'summarize the advantages of his product while holding a burning match'.

DEFINING IDEA...

The sale begins when the customer says yes.

~ HARVEY MCKAY,
AUTHOR AND SPEAKER

In the age of counter-terrorist operations, the right to stop and search and potential suicide bombers, that might just get you arrested. But Bettger does suggest that, where possible, you get your prospective client to write down the summary points, 'Number one...', 'Number two...' etc. This active participation can do wonders for a positive end result.

The third rule is the 'magic phrase': 'How do you like that?' Bettger seems convinced that by asking this question your prospect will agree that it looks good and enthuse about your offering. Again I'm not convinced that would work in today's cynical society. Sadly, we are no longer that bothered about being rude to salespeople!

If your company offers a range of products, Bettger suggests that salespeople are encouraged to help their prospects to make a choice between two or more options rather than between 'yes' or 'no'. Finding ways to encourage your prospect to say positive things – even if it's just to confirm their name and address – will help to gather positive momentum.

'Welcome objections' is rule four. Rule five encourages you to ask 'why?' so that you can appreciate your customer's perspective. Once a prospect answers your question, go on to ask 'And in addition to that?' so you can get to the real issues and address them.

Asking prospects to write their name on the application form is rule six, although that is often done for you now. One word of warning, however – make sure your data entry people are proficient and English is their first language so they can spot the obvious mistakes. I always remember a friend of mine in Australia called Paul Buckingham; on certain databases he was entered as Pork Buckingham. Apart from providing me with hours of entertainment it's safe to assume Paul never bought anything from a company that thought he was a variety of meat – even after repeated assurances that he wasn't. Pre-filling the order form can be convenient and allow you to create the positive momentum you require for a successful sale, but be sure the information and spelling is correct otherwise you could shoot yourself in the foot!

Bettger suggests that the final rule is to get the cheque there are then: 'Don't be afraid of money,' he says, adding, 'I've never had a man cancel an order when he's paid something on account.'

HERE'S AN IDEA FOR YOU...

Try and get your prospect to confirm at least five things before you get to the final close. You need to ask questions to which there is a strong likelihood that your prospective client will say 'yes'. Find ways to have them agree with you throughout the presentation and use this positive momentum to direct you towards a successful close.

46 POSITIVE EXPECTATION

Bettger quite clearly believed in a positive attitude. He kept cards summarising his seven rules of the close with him at all times and across the top of each card were the words, 'This is going to be the best interview I ever had…'

Along the lines of Émile Coué's famous affirmation, 'Every day, in every way, I am getting better and better', these words helped to affirm his attitude prior to a meeting. Since he wrote the book in 1947 science has shown us that our intentions, attitude and expectations really do have an impact on an outcome.

DEFINING IDEA...

High expectations are the key to everything.

~ SAM WALTON,
FOUNDER OF WAL-MART

One of the most famous and demonstrable impacts of belief on outcome are placebos. There are many documented cases of placebo medicine at work. In one a patient suffering from very advanced cancer of the lymph nodes was given an experimental drug. It had miraculous effects. Later news stories appeared that refuted the drug's effectiveness and the patient suffered a relapse. His doctor, Bruno Klopfer, was so desperate that he told his patient that he had secured a new double-strength drug – but it was actually a placebo. Klopfer reported that the patient's tumours 'melted like snowballs on a hot stove'. The only explanation was his belief in his doctor and in the new drug.

More recently, in 2002, a Baylor School of Medicine study was published in the *New England Journal of Medicine* that demonstrated the power of the placebo effect – this time in surgery. Dr Bruce Moseley, who believed that 'all good surgeons know there is no placebo effect in surgery', wanted, nevertheless, to assess what part of knee surgery was causing an improvement. The subjects were split into three groups. In the first Mosley shaved the damaged cartilage in the knee. In the second he flushed the material which was thought to cause inflammation out of the knee. And in the third, placebo, group he made three standard incisions and then talked and acted as though he was doing the operation – even splashing salt water to mimic the sound of the knee-washing procedure. After forty minutes Moseley sewed up the incisions. All three groups were given the same aftercare and physiotherapy programme.

Those who received the surgery improved as expected. What shocked Dr Moseley to the core was that the placebo group improved by as much as the other two groups – so much so that he suggested, 'My skill as a surgeon had no benefit on these patients. The entire benefit of the surgery for osteoarthritis of the knee was the placebo effect.'

If belief can cure cancer and fix dodgy knees, then a positive attitude and expectation may do wonders for your sales success.

HERE'S AN IDEA FOR YOU...

Take the time before every meeting to get yourself in the right frame of mind. Imagine what it will be like in the meeting; imagine how you will feel when it goes really well and your prospect agrees to place a huge order that will make you loads of money and give you umpteen new contacts and referrals. Get into the habit of expecting the best. It may not always guarantee you success, but expecting the worst will guarantee failure.

47 ASSESS YOUR FAILURES

Bettger says that if, after approaching all your interviews or selling situations expecting the best, the inevitable happens and you bomb then you shouldn't just ignore it or write it off to the other person's fault. Using the seven rules of the close Bettger immediately checked what he'd done wrong.

Being able to assess failures honestly so you can learn from them and improve over time is one of the hallmarks of success in any walk of life.

DEFINING IDEA...

My great concern is not whether you have failed but whether you are content with your failure.

~ ABRAHAM LINCOLN

In psychology this area of research is called 'Attribution Theory'. Attribution theory suggests that people's explanations for success and failure are attributed to either internal or external factors, and it is this attribution that dictates future expectations of success. The original framework for attribution theory was based on the work of Bernard Weiner who suggested three dimensions of attribution:

• Locus: was it caused by internal or external factors?

• Stability: did the cause remain the same, or did it change?

• Responsibility: could the person control the cause?

Being able to immediately assess your performance from this perspective can help you to make adjustments in the future and not dampen your spirits. There is no point engaging in what is known as 'self-serving bias'. This is the tendency to attribute success to internal factors, such as knowledge and effort, and failures to uncontrollable external causes such as bad luck, your prospect's mood or the traffic.

How we handle failure is not just a test of character, it is apparently part of character. Psychologist Michael F. Scheier reported in the *Journal of Personality and Social Psychology* that optimists tend to respond to disappointment by formulating a plan of action and asking other people for help and advice. Pessimists, on the other hand, try to forget the whole thing or assume there was nothing they could have done differently.

However, Dr Martin Seligman, another psychologist, wanted to explore this idea further to give those natural pessimists a little more control. Seligman noted that pessimists tended to attribute poor results or bad events to some personal defect that will plague them forever (he called this their explanatory style), thus developing 'learned helplessness'. In one of his most illuminating research experiments he studied the Harvard graduating class of 1939–1944. After returning from the war and having physical examinations every five years, Seligman stated that, 'The men's explanatory style at age 25 predicted their health at 65. Around age 45 the health of the pessimists started to deteriorate more quickly.'

Seligman went on to develop positive psychology, the study of optimal human functioning to help people live a more optimistic existence regardless of their inherent explanatory style. Bettger encourages us to use failure as the springboard to success.

HERE'S AN IDEA FOR YOU...

Go over a failure straight away. Focus only on what you could have done better. Role play how you should have conducted the interview immediately – this sends a message to your brain about how it should have been done. Athletes do this all the time with shadow play, where they immediately run through a shot again after an error. Create five actionable, specific things you could do differently next time – and do them.

48 THOUGHTS TEND TO PASS INTO ACTION

Bettger is wondering about the psychology of a particular close. On going back for a second interview, he ignored the protests of the client and put the application form in front of him and a pen in his hand. He thought it 'crowded out all the reasons against signing until thought passed into action'.

I'm not sure his particular method would work today without you getting thrown out of the office of the person concerned, but what I am 100% sure about is that thought tends to pass into action. Whatever we think about translates into action – or inaction. What we are now appreciating is that those thoughts have an impact on the neural circuitry of the brain. What we think actually affects our biology and the speed at which we learn new skills.

DEFINING IDEA...

I've discovered that numerous peak performers use the skill of mental rehearsal of visualization. They mentally run through important events before they happen.

~ DR CHARLES GARFIELD.
AUTHOR OF PEAK PERFORMANCE

In 1995 a study was published in the *Journal of Neurophysiology* that demonstrated the power of thought and visualisation, and how it can alter the neural networks in the brain just as much as actual physical effort. Research volunteers were split into four groups. The first group had to memorise a specific one-handed five-finger sequence on the piano which they had to practise every day for two hours over a five-day period. The second group was asked to play the piano without any instruction. They played randomly for two hours every day for the five days. The third group never touched a piano at all but were given the opportunity to observe what was taught to the first group until they had also memorised it. They were then to mentally rehearse the sequence for two hours every day for five days. The final group was the control group and they didn't do anything.

At the end of the study the researchers used a technique called transcranial magnetic stimulation to measure any brain changes that had taken place. The group that had only thought about the piano-playing technique and visualised themselves doing it showed almost the same expansion and neural network development in the same specific area of their brain as the group who had played the piano and done the five-finger exercise. They even demonstrated greater proficiency than the second group – people who had actually played a piano!

This is known as Hebbian learning. Visualisation allows us to physically change our brain to support improved performance. Nerve cells that fire together, wire together.

If you can stimulate these neural connections through mental rehearsal then they will strengthen in the same way that a physical muscle will strengthen if you lift weights. There are therefore two ways to create these neural connections – by physically doing the task and by thinking about doing the task. If you want to be successful in sales, therefore, you might want to start visualising that success.

HERE'S AN IDEA FOR YOU...

Set targets about what you want to achieve, fully engage in what success will mean to you. What will you wear? What will you drive? Where will you live? Inject as much emotional energy into the visualisation, really feel how you would feel and let your imagination run wild. Run through the visualisation in your mind every night and morning.

49 DISCIPLINE

Bettger talks of a man called Dick Campbell who said, 'In this world, we either discipline ourselves, or we are disciplined by the world.' Having a plan and the discipline to implement it, alter it where necessary and then keep on working it is a necessary part of success in any field of endeavour.

For those readers who get niggled about inconsistency or missing pieces of information you'll be glad to read that this chapter explains the importance of Robert B. Cialdini's sixth and final principle that directs human behaviour – commitment and consistency.

DEFINING IDEA...
Some people regard discipline as a chore. For me, it is a kind of order that sets me free to fly.
– JULIE ANDREWS

Cialdini states this to be 'our nearly obsessive desire to be (and to appear) consistent with what we have already done. Once we make a choice or take a stand, we will encounter personal and interpersonal pressures to behave consistently with that commitment.'

If we are disciplined in our efforts we generate a commitment and consistency that keeps us on task and which is also appealing to prospects. If we always do what we say we will do, and consistently keep in touch and help others, then we will be successful.

This potency of commitment and consistency can be seen at work where people write down their goals. That act of writing them down makes them active, and research has shown that active commitment is more powerful by far than passive commitment.

Social scientists Delia Cioffi and Randy Garner solicited collage students to volunteer their time for a charitable organisation. Half were told that if they wanted to volunteer they had to fill out a form (active commitment) and the other half were told that if they wanted to volunteer they had to leave the part of the form saying they didn't want to volunteer blank (passive commitment). The percentage of people from each group who agreed to volunteer was about the same, but there was a huge disparity between those who actually turned up to do their voluntary work. Only 17% of those who passively agreed to volunteer turned up – versus 49% of those who actively committed.

So actively commit to your goals, write them down and be disciplined about their execution. You can also use this principle to engage a prospect; if they write something down they are much more likely to follow through on the commitment.

If you are in any doubt about the need for discipline and the ramifications of indiscipline, then consider the global recession which was brought on primarily by a fundamental lack of discipline in the banking sector. Or what about the politicians' expenses scandal in the UK? I always thought they had their proverbial snouts in the trough but to realise that many were immersed up to the ears is a sad indictment on British politics. Unfortunately the world is not just disciplining those who screwed up – we are all suffering.

HERE'S AN IDEA FOR YOU...

If you want action in your sales meetings or are a sales manager and want to help your people to hit their targets, have them write them down and announce to the group what business they are going to generate in the coming month. This public commitment will activate their internal drive to be consistent with that declaration.

50 FOSTER INDIFFERENCE

According to Bettger, one of the things that made Babe Ruth such an outstanding baseball player was that he fostered indifference in the outcome. Regardless of the result, 'The expression on his face was exactly like the one he wore on his first two trips, when he had taken a razzing.'

DEFINING IDEA...

Cultivate a little the don't-care habit; don't worry about what people think. This will endear you to others and make you liked and loved all the more.

~ DR LOUIS E. BISCH, PSYCHIATRIST

Bettger was watching Babe Ruth play in the summer of 1927 in front of 35,000 wildly excited baseball fans packed into Shibe Park, Philadelphia. He had been struck out twice, once missing the ball so hard that he swung himself off his feet and landed face down in the dirt, and the crowd were giving him 'the "razzberry" – and good!' Yet his expression never changed. He smiled a little smile to the crowd, doffed his cap, dusted himself off and got ready for the next pitch.

Only this time his bat connected and the ball was never seen again. It cleared the scoreboard and the houses across the street in one of the longest hits ever made in the history of baseball. As he trotted around the bases he smiled his little smile and doffed his cap to the crowd.

Babe Ruth had mastered the art of indifference.

Bettger suggests that, 'When you try too hard and become overanxious you look bad. You are bad. Yes, keep going, but don't be afraid to lose today. Today is not going to make or break you. You can't bat .300 every day. The crowd loves a good loser; everyone despises a quitter.'

Being able to control your emotions in a particular situation gives you strength and poise. No one enjoys confrontation or difficulty, and there will always be days that don't go right for you. But none of it means anything except the meaning you ascribe to it.

Babe Ruth could have been embarrassed and humiliated as the crowd heckled his failure. He could have made it mean that he wasn't playing well or that perhaps his career was coming to an end. Instead he chose to treat every new swing as a new opportunity to do what he loved – play ball and win or lose.

What makes human beings different from the other animals is the pre-frontal cortex of the brain. This is the home to our decision-making skills, creativity and free will. We have choice and it's our responsibility to exercise that choice towards success. Fostering indifference to the outcome is one way in which we can do that.

Bettger suggests that, 'Whenever a salesman gets out of the habit of seeing enough prospects, he loses his sense of indifference.' He encourages us not to be discouraged by failure, to maintain consistent effort throughout and 'give old-man law of averages sufficient chance to work for you'.

HERE'S AN IDEA FOR YOU...

You do have to give 100% effort and try every time, but don't be attached to the outcome. Foster a sense of indifference – but only to the outcome. Do your best, keep making the calls and booking appointments. Resolve not to rise to irritations or failures any more than you would gloat in successes. Maintain a steady composure.

51 HAVE COURAGE

As would be expected in a book on sales, Bettger talks a great deal about failure and recommends courage and perseverance as the remedy. Everyone has setbacks. Few people had as many as Abraham Lincoln and yet his courage and perseverance resulted in him becoming one of the most influential US Presidents.

DEFINING IDEA...

Our doubts are traitors, and make us lose the good we oft might win, by fearing to attempt.

– WILLIAM SHAKESPEARE

Apparently, in 1915 Ty Cobb set a record of stealing 96 bases. Seven years later Max Carey set the second-best record of 51 bases stolen. If you were to look at their averages, then Carey stole 96% of those he attempted against 71% of Cobb's. But Cobb was the winner by far because he tried eighty-one more times than Carey did – he risked failure eighty-one times more. Ty Cobb refused to fear failure. He had the courage to try more often than the others, and that's what history remembers.

Doubt has the opposite effect to belief. And if placebos with no medical properties can cure disease, then 'nocebos' are just as powerful – only they are destructive.

When a mind is engaged in negative suggestion and this damages overall health, it is known as the nocebo effect. Here's an example. In 1974, Nashville physician Clifton Meador had a patient suffering from cancer of the oesophagus, a condition thought at the time to be 100% fatal. Everyone 'knew' he would die – including the patient. Sure enough, he met everyone's expectations and died. What did come as a surprise was that the autopsy showed very little cancer in his body. Meador has been haunted ever since – had the patient died because he believed he would die?

Someone else who probably died as a result of the nocebo effect was Karl Wallenda. Wallenda was a legendary tightrope walker, famous for performing death-defying stunts without any safety net. On 18 July 1970, a sixty-five year-old Wallenda performed a high-wire walk across the Tallulah Gorge while 30,000 people watched. He performed two headstands as he crossed the quarter-mile gap – still without a net!

Eight years later, at the age of seventy-three, he attempted to walk between two towers of the ten-storey Condado Plaza Hotel in San Juan, Puerto Rico on a wire 37 metres above the ground. Tragically, he fell to his death. Following the accident, his wife was reported to say that, 'For months prior to his performance, he thought about nothing else. But for the first time, he didn't see himself succeeding. He saw himself falling.' His courage failed him and his belief in himself wavered – although at least he died doing what he loved.

Bettger ends by encouraging us to, 'Keep going! Each week, each month, you are improving. One day soon, you will find a way to do the thing that today looks impossible... Courage is not the absence of fear, it is the conquest of it.'

HERE'S AN IDEA FOR YOU...

Make a conscious choice about how you are going to approach each sale, do your research and plan your approach. Visualise it going well and be prepared to handle objections – but after that don't dwell on what might happen. Your mind can so easily turn against you, erode your confidence and dispel your courage.

52 FRANKLIN'S THIRTEEN SUBJECTS

It's clear from the number of references to him that Bettger was an admirer of Benjamin Franklin. According to Bettger, Franklin attributed his success and happiness to the fostering of thirteen traits and wrote prolifically on the subjects he laid out as necessary for success.

DEFINING IDEA...

Commit to CANI! – Constant and Never-ending Improvement.
~ ANTHONY ROBBINS

We are asked to remember that Benjamin Franklin was a scientist and his plan for cultivation was, therefore, scientific. 'Reject it,' warns Bettger, 'and you reject one of the most practical ideas ever offered you.'

Franklin's thirteen subjects to cultivate for success were (with my interpretations in brackets):

1. Temperance (don't eat or drink too much); 2. Silence (shut up if you can't say anything helpful); 3. Order (let all things have their place); 4. Resolution (do what you say and say what you do); 5. Frugality (don't spend what you haven't got); 6. Industry (be useful); 7. Sincerity (don't lie); 8. Justice (don't cheat); 9. Moderation (too much of anything is a bad thing); 10. Cleanliness (wash!); 11. Tranquillity (don't sweat the small stuff); 12. Chastity (don't waste your energy on too much nooky); 13. Humility (be kind and tolerant).

Franklin dedicated one consecutive week to each subject: 'In this way he was able to go through his entire list of thirteen weeks, and repeat the process four times a year.' I wonder if Mrs Franklin was put out at week twelve, or relieved!

For the purposes of mastering the art of selling, Bettger modified Franklin's list to include:

1. Enthusiasm; 2. Order: self-organisation; 3. Think in terms of other's interests; 4. Questions; 5. Key issues; 6. Silence: listen; 7. Sincerity: deserve confidence; 8. Knowledge of my business; 9. Appreciation and praise; 10. Smile: happiness; 11. Remember names and faces; 12. Service and prospecting; 13. Closing the sale: action.

Bettger made up pocket reminders of each of his chosen subjects, together with a brief explanation of what each one meant. As Franklin suggested, he focused on one subject for one week, carrying that card with him at all times. He would look at the card when he had a spare moment and be reminded to foster that trait. After he completed the first thirteen weeks he would start again with the first subject and continue throughout the year. He says 'Each week, I gained a clearer understanding of my subject. It got down deeper inside of me. My business became more interesting. It became exciting!'

Bettger closes by saying how much he values Franklin's idea: 'I know. I know what it did for me. I know it can do the same for anyone who will try it. It's not an easy way. There is no easy way. But it is a sure way.'

HERE'S AN IDEA FOR YOU...

Brainstorm thirteen subjects of your own that you feel would greatly assist your selling success – or any other area of your life that you wish to improve (or use either Bettger's or Franklin's). Write your chosen subjects out on pocket reminder cards and carry them with you. Insert the subject into each week of your diary so you know which subject you are working on at any given time.

CONCLUSION

Writing a sales book that is new is a challenge, even if you are writing a modernisation of an old classic. I have, without a doubt, wandered off topic a few times. Hopefully you will forgive me that and have found the book enjoyable and interesting, if not a little quirky at times.

The reason I covered some of the topics in the way I have is because I believe that what goes on in the six inches between your ears is far more important to your success than any tip, technique, sharp suit or embossed business card. And that's why I've explored the odd rabbit hole in this book. If you would like to know more about the power of thought then you may enjoy one of my other titles in this series, on Napoleon Hill's *Think and Grow Rich*.

If you are reading this book then you probably have at least fifty books on sales in your library. Erring on the side of caution, you've read half a dozen of them cover to cover. You're also probably in sales already or want some new ideas on how you may be able to improve your batting average. Thing is, you probably already know everything there is to know about selling. And you almost certainly know more than I do about selling.

Selling was always one of those subjects that brought me out in a cold sweat. So much so that at one point in my career prior to writing I felt I needed to tackle my demons and went into telesales for a while. I thought the best way to conquer my fear was to face it. A noble idea in principle, but I hated every minute of it. Sorry if that wasn't very inspiring!

Before I was a writer I worked in marketing on both the client and agency side; I used to make that direct mail you hate with a passion and throw in the bin. I remember vividly being asked to attend sales training courses and being dragged kicking and screaming into business development discussions.

Then I became a writer. Like anyone who has ventured out on their own I realised that selling my services was as much a part of my job as writing but, strangely enough, selling became quite straightforward. I'm lucky in that most of my business comes from word of mouth and referral; the Internet also offers some fantastic opportunities. But what I've come to understand is that honesty, sincerity and a genuine belief in what you are selling makes the whole process far less daunting.

I am very grateful for the messages in Bettger's book. I came across his words long before I read all of his book and one overarching principle has become the bedrock of how I operate and has profoundly shaped my business and who I am as a writer: find out what other people want and help them get it.

Bettger closes the book with a chapter he calls, 'Let's you and I have a heart-to-heart talk.' In it, he warns 'you haven't got that much time'. 'I don't know how old you are,' he says, 'but let's assume, for example, you are about thirty-five. It's later than you think. It won't be long before you are forty. And once you pass forty, time goes so fast.'

He warns against inertia and rightly points out that reading books alone will not change your life and improve your results – action is the only thing that can do that.

And don't panic – they tell me forty is the new thirty!

REFERENCE MATERIAL

IDEA 2:
Psycho-Cybernetics, Maxwell Maltz, p. xii

IDEA 12:
Evolve your Brain: The Science of Changing Your Mind, Joe Dispenza DC, p.123

IDEA 21:
On Writing Well, 4th edition, William Zinsser, p. 148

IDEA 22:
The Biology of Belief: Unleashing the Power of Consciousness, Matter and Miracles, Bruce H. Lipton PhD, p. 97, p. 136

IDEA 24:
The Seven-Day Weekend, Ricardo Semler, p. 7

IDEA 27:
Yes! 50 Secrets from the Science of Persuasion, Noah J. Goldstein PhD, Steve J. Martin and Robert B. Cialdini PhD, pp. 101–102

IDEA 28:
The Biology of Belief: Unleashing the Power of Consciousness, Matter and Miracles, Bruce H. Lipton PhD, p. 69

IDEA 29:
A User's Guide to the Brain John J. Ratey, p.229.
'Paper reveals Ruth Padel's "smear" email', Alison Flood, *Guardian*, 27 May 2009

IDEA 31:
Influence: Science and Practice, Robert B. Cialdini PhD, p. 95

IDEA 33:
Yes! 50 Secrets from the Science of Persuasion, Noah J. Goldstein PhD, Steve J. Martin and Robert B. Cialdini PhD, pp. 127–128

IDEA 34:
Synchrodestiny: Harnessing the Infinite Power of Coincidence to Create Miracles, Deepak Chopra, p. 54

IDEA 37:
Yes! 50 Secrets from the Science of Persuasion, Noah J. Goldstein PhD, Steve J. Martin and Robert B. Cialdini PhD, p. 73

IDEA 39:
Selling to VITO – the Very Important Top Officer: Increase your commissions by getting appointments with top decision makers today, Anthony Parinello, pp. 34, 116–117

IDEA 40:
A User's Guide to the Brain, John J. Ratey, p. 20

IDEA 46:
The Biology of Belief: Unleashing the Power of Consciousness, Matter and Miracles, Bruce H. Lipton PhD, pp. 108–109
Getting Well Again, O. Carl Simonton MD, Stephanie Matthews-Simonton and James L Creighton, p. 26

IDEA 47:
Research affirms power of positive thinking, Daniel Goleman, *New York Times*, 3 Feb 1987

IDEA 49:
Influence: Science and Practice, Robert B. Cialdini PhD, pp. 50–51
Yes! 50 Secrets from the Science of Persuasion, Noah J. Goldstein PhD, Steve J. Martin and Robert B. Cialdini PhD, p. 67

IDEA 51:
The Biology of Belief: Unleashing the Power of Consciousness, Matter and Miracles, Bruce H. Lipton PhD, p. 112

INDEX

Made in the USA
Lexington, KY
26 October 2011